faerie magick

Dedication

This book is dedicated to Ian David Weatherill, my friend and companion of the Round Table!

With love from Marie

faerie magick

harness the power
of natural magick

Marie Bruce

quantum
LONDON • NEW YORK • TORONTO • SYDNEY

quantum

An imprint of W. Foulsham & Co. Ltd
The Publishing House, Bennetts Close, Cippenham, Slough, Berkshire, SL1 5AP, England

Foulsham books can be found in all good bookshops or direct from www.foulsham.com

ISBN 0-572-03123-8

Cover artwork by Jurgen Ziewe

A CIP record for this book is available from the British Library

Illustrations by Ruth Murray and Hayley Fancesconi

Neither the editors of W. Foulsham & Co. Ltd nor the author nor the publisher take responsibility for any possible consequences from any treatment, procedure, test, exercise, action or application of medication or preparation by any person reading or following the information in this book. The publication of this book does not constitute the practice of medicine, and this book does not attempt to replace any diet or instructions from your doctor. The author and publisher advise the reader to check with a doctor before administering any medication or undertaking any course of treatment or exercise.

Printed in Great Britain by St. Edmundsbury Press, Bury St. Edmunds, Suffolk.

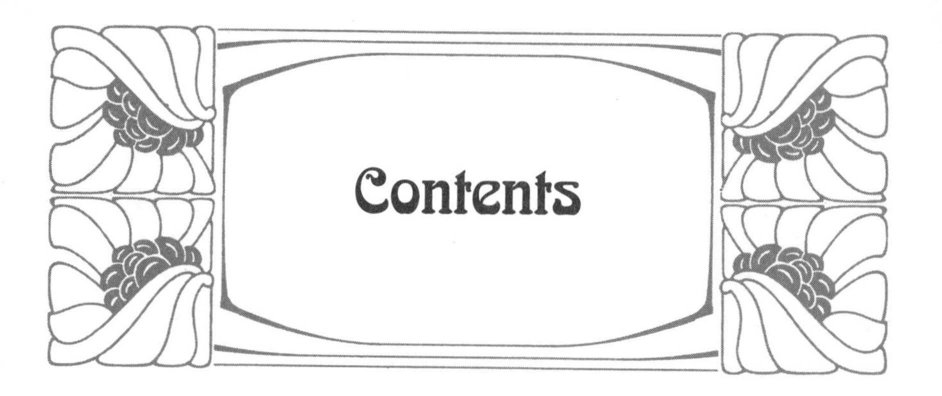
Contents

Spell Singer

Tell it to the moon in the darkest hour;
Tell it to the starlight, tell it to the starlight.
Sing to the Goddess and feel your power;
You can make your dreams come true.
Tell it to the sun in the daylight hours;
Tell it to the sunlight, tell it to the sunlight.
Sing of the Earth and feel Her power;
Sing of the skies so blue.
Dance in the fall of a summer shower;
Tell it to the rain drops, tell it to the rain drops.
Call on the Old Gods and feel their power;
Feel the power deep in you.
Sing to the clouds and sing to the flowers;
Tell it to the treetops, tell it to the treetops.
Welcome the rebirth of pagan power.
Come and join the circle too.
Dance in the dark of the witching hour.
Tell it to the moonbeams, sing a song of your dreams;
Dance round the blaze of the witch's fire.
Free the magick inside you!

Do You Believe in Faeries?

Faeries are both timeless and universal. They form a part of the folklore of all cultures and all ages, and tales about them are many and varied.

Most of you will be familiar with the popular image of the faerie, complete with flower-petal dress and gauzy butterfly wings. But did you know that these images personify a very real life force and that this lasting image came into being through humankind's need to understand and relate to the wild, untameable energies of nature? And did you know that you can call on these energies to help you overcome a challenge in life and attune with the natural world around you?

Faeries are real. They do exist, and witches and magickal practitioners have been invoking their powers for centuries. Here in this book you will learn all about the true faeries – the elemental powers of nature – and how to work with them. You will also discover which faeries are most in tune with your birth sign, the magickal significance of well-known faerie tales and how to create powerful faerie thought forms. Plus, you will learn how to create a variety of beautiful faerie altars and shrines, and how to put together your own unique Faerie Grimoire, a book of spells and rituals dedicated to the enchanted faerie realm.

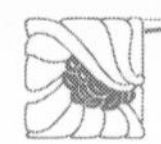

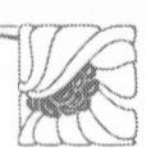

All you need is an open mind, a loving heart and a few basic tools, and you can welcome these captivating beings of light and joy into your life. So without further ado let's take our first step through the portal into the Enchanted Realm ... in perfect love and perfect trust, with a magickal pinch of faerie dust!

Blessed be!
Morgana

Spellbound!

Once upon a time, an ordinary person in the ordinary world picked up a book about faeries and discovered that life can be truly magickal!

Welcome to my little book of faerie spells. In opening this book you have entered a world of magick, where anything – and I mean anything – can happen! If you let it. Here you are going to learn the mysteries of the Enchanted Realm. You will discover the vast power of elementals and empower yourself in the process. Indeed, you may even transform your own life into something of a magickal faerie tale along the way!

This book will show you how to discover your own personal bliss and live each day with a sense of joy and rapture, while making the very most of the magickal power you hold deep within you. For you are a magickal being in your own right. You have the power to make things happen, and you can change your life for the better, starting right now! Want to know more? Then read on and discover the secrets of faerie spellcasting ...

Of witches and faeries

Faerie magick is for all people of all ages. It is a simple form of magick and so is perfect for beginners and those new to witchcraft and spellcasting, yet because it is so effective, faerie power is often used by adept magickal practitioners too. Anyone with a genuine interest in magick and faeries can work effective faerie spells and can begin to create the kind of life they truly want and deserve.

Witches and faeries are inextricably linked. Both are found in folklore and faerie tale throughout the various cultures of the globe. Most myths and legends hold within them a kernel of truth, and faerie stories are no exception to this rule. Beneath the surface of the bedtime stories of childhood there is the underlying magickal truth of a natural power just waiting to be tapped into and used. Storybook witches actually have their roots in the old village wise women and pagan priestesses of the past. These were the women who made healing potions, divined the future, cast love spells and performed fertility rites. Over time, the power of the wise woman was ridiculed, and her popular image in folklore became that of the wicked witch.

A similar thing occurred with faeries, which are today widely considered to be pretty, harmless creatures invented to delight little girls. However, the origins of the modern picture book faerie lie in the elemental spirits and the vast power of nature's life force. Today's magickal practitioners still use this life force in their spells and rituals, just as the priestesses and wise women of the past did. The practice of drawing upon these natural energies is known as faerie magick or elemental magick.

The changing face of witchcraft

The face of witchcraft is well and truly changing. The stereotypical old hag is slowly being replaced by the more popular image of the witch as a young, feisty, sexy and independent female. This pretty witch is just as strong and just as powerful as her predecessor, yet she is somehow more socially acceptable! She teaches that witches can be smart, beautiful, cool, hip and trendy; that they can be career-minded, go-getting individuals and high achievers; that they are often clever, witty, and intelligent; and that, ultimately, there are no limits to female power.

This enchanting 'witch babe' is appealing to a whole new generation of magickal practitioners and wannabe witches. Women of all ages, from pre-teens to senior citizens, are discovering for themselves the positive message of female empowerment that witchcraft teaches. All of a sudden it's cool to be Crafty!

As a result, witchcraft has probably never been more popular than it is today – it's both the newest thing and the oldest trick in the book!

The truth about witchcraft

As a gentle, tolerant, earth-loving spirituality, witchcraft is attuned to the natural energies of the Enchanted Realm – which is why faerie magick is so effective. Witchcraft does work but, unlike the faerie stories of childhood, I cannot promise absolutely that you will live happily ever after. Sometimes life sends hard knocks to try us and to make us more resilient. While witchcraft won't save you from such knocks, it will give you the power and the strength you need to get through the tough times, enabling you to bounce back more quickly and making you stronger and more powerful than ever.

As witchcraft becomes more popular, some people are being drawn to it for the wrong reasons. They may be jumping on the bandwagon and following the crowd, or they may think that life as a witch will be a breeze. It won't. In fact, things tends to get worse before they get better when magick is involved! This is because magick works to balance out your life. So if you're new to witchcraft, expect a few hiccups in the early days. Magick will strip away anything that isn't for your greater good or is causing you some kind of imbalance. This could mean the ending of a relationship, a health scare or some other kind of wake-up call. The severity of your own wake-up call depends entirely on how unbalanced you have become. If your life is 'way out of whack', so to speak, be prepared for some serious consequences when you begin to work magick! Otherwise, a gentle tug here and there will be all it takes to enable you to regain equilibrium in your life.

Magick of any kind should never be viewed as a quick fix. It's easy to pretend that waving a magick wand will make your life perfect, but the reality is that magick is more of a kick-start and a power boost to the actions you take yourself. You must take responsibility for your own life – mistakes and all!

Using magick and witchcraft can help steer your life in the direction you most want to go, but it won't do all the work for you. For example, if you are constantly running up credit card and catalogue debts and amalgamating loans, all the abundance spells in the world won't help you until you learn to stop spending what you don't have. Only when you have accepted responsibility for the problem and changed your actions accordingly will magick be of any help in managing the debts you have accumulated and building a pocket of financial security and wealth for yourself.

That said, magick does somehow ensure that things fall into place.

Things may not always work out exactly as you expected, but when magick is involved, things will always turn out for the best. It may not necessarily seem that way at the time, but you will eventually come to see that this is so. Bear this in mind if things seem to be going awry!

So what's in it for me?

Glad you asked! And the answer is – a lot, actually! When you bring magick into your life, your life in turn becomes magickal. Each day is an adventure, and serendipity (meaning a fortunate accident) becomes almost commonplace. All of a sudden you seem to find yourself in the right place, at the right time, surrounded by the right people. Life introduces you to people who are perfect for who you are and what you need, and you in turn, are perfect for them. This could be in your romantic, your personal or your professional life, but you will always benefit from a very happy circumstance – it's kismet!

Witches and magickal practitioners know that there really is no such thing as coincidence. Everything happens for a reason. This means that everything that happens to you, everything you have endured and experienced in your life so far, has a purpose. It also means that you didn't come across this book by accident! You are meant to read these words and you have been picked out by the universe to become one of my magickal readers and students!

Hopefully, you will also choose to act upon the teachings in this book and change your life for the better.

Which brings us to a few more questions frequently asked by neophyte witches: can magick really change your life? Can casting a few spells really have an effect on your daily existence? Is magick real? At the risk of sounding like a popular shampoo advert ... Yes! Yes! Yes!

Magick is a tremendous force, which, when properly directed, can totally transform your life if that is what you wish. It can make your dreams come true, helping you to realise ambitions and goals, it can turn your idea of an ideal relationship into a reality and it can inspire you to approach life in a completely new way, at the same time giving you a magickal edge over any competition you may come up against. And at times the effects of your spellcastings will undoubtedly surprise you! This is because magick will always work for your highest good, giving you what you most need, which is not always the same as what you most want! Generally speaking, though, such a surprise will prove to be a pleasant one!

Successful spellcasting

As with anything else, there is a technique to casting effective and successful spells. If it were simply a matter of lighting a candle and muttering a few words from a spell book, wouldn't everyone be doing it? True magick is not so easy as that. It takes time, effort, skill and concentration to cast the kind of spell that gets results.

Many new practitioners fail in their first attempts at magick because they are unfocused. You must focus completely on the intended outcome throughout the duration of the spell in order for the magick to be successful. Part of focus is maintaining a strong, clear visualisation of your magickal goal, seeing it in your mind's eye as if it has already happened. If you are working a spell to pass your driving test, for example, you would visualise the examiner congratulating you on passing. Visualisation is something we all do quite naturally; the trick is to apply this familiar skill to your magick, seeing the positive manifestation of the spell.

Maintaining a strong focus is perhaps the most difficult aspect of spellcasting, so don't worry if you find it challenging. Just remember that practice makes perfect and it will get easier with time.

It is also important not to impose boundaries on yourself and your magick. By this I mean that you should allow your spells to manifest in their own way. If you cast for a new TV, don't be overly specific, stating which store the TV should come from and so on, as this places a boundary on manifestation. Be clear about what you want from your new TV and then let the magick shop around for you! In this way you will get exactly what you want at the best deal the universe has to offer!

Sometimes spells manifest in unexpected and surprising ways. It may seem as if there is some trickster out there who is playing games and messing around with your life. On occasions you may get exactly what you wanted and needed but from a source that you hadn't even considered. If this happens, don't pretend that the magick didn't work, dismissing such a manifestation out of hand. Remember that everything in magick happens for a reason, and just allow yourself to go with the flow for a while. Test the magick out by trying the manifestation on for size. Just live with it for a while. If you do this, you will in all probability come to see that your spell has manifested in such a way as to be for your highest good – and could even prove to be life-changing! Such surprising manifestations are a joy to experience. At such times in your life, you may begin to understand the true power of the natural forces you are working with. Witches have a saying that goes 'in perfect love and perfect trust'. This basically means that everything we do in our magickal lives we do in the spirit of love and trust. Trust in the magick! It won't let you down.

The rules of spellcasting

There are certain rules that must be adhered to if you don't want to find yourself in a magickal mess of consequences! For every action there is a reaction, and magick is no exception to this rule. Every spell you cast, every ritual and magickal act you perform, will alter your reality in some way, creating a ripple effect within your life. This in turn will subtly alter the reality of the people around you, which is why working magick of any kind carries such a huge weight of responsibility. It has the power to change lives! From the moment you picked up this book, positive change became a possibility for you, and if you act on the information held within these pages, your life will almost certainly improve to some degree.

So what are the rules of effective spellcasting?

The Wiccan Rede

The Wiccan Rede is perhaps the most important rule in magick. It states:

An' it harm none, do what you will.

This is in fact a variation on an ancient spiritual law, meaning treat others as you would wish to be treated yourself. The key words are 'harm none'. Every single spell you work must be cast 'with harm to none', and this includes yourself and the animal kingdom.

All the spells in this book adhere to this rule, and – being faerie spells – they are all very gentle and positive in their nature. When you begin to write and create your own spells and rituals, you must make absolutely certain that your magick harms no-one in any way. This includes using magick to gain control over a person or to influence someone for your own ends. Misusing magick to make a specific person fall in love with you, for example, goes against the Wiccan Rede and could have serious consequences.

Contrary to popular belief, witches do not cast spells on other people. We cast them around ourselves, effectively magnetising what we require in a natural and gentle way. This is why effective magick is often put down to coincidence, but, as I've already mentioned, witches don't believe in coincidence. We believe that everything happens for a reason. So when your first spell manifests in your life, don't put it down to coincidence. Treat it as an affirmation of your personal magickal power and give yourself a pat on the back for a job well done!

Although the 'harm none' rule is very basic, and could even be said to be common sense, it isn't always easy to follow. There will be times in your life when you are tempted to break the rules, go against the Rede, and cast a negative spell out of anger, jealousy or spite. You're only human after all, and it's quite natural to feel angry sometimes. Just be aware that if you do break the Rede and work magick to cause someone harm, it will undoubtedly backfire on you, and you will eventually have to deal with the consequences. You've been warned!

Magickal practitioners have to think very carefully before casting a spell, asking themselves questions such as: who will this spell directly affect? Who will it indirectly affect? Am I prepared to accept the consequences of this spell and its manifestation in my life? Is there any possibility that this spell could have a negative effect on anyone? And so on.

If there is any possibility that your spell could cause harm, don't do it! Try to work around the problem, rewording the spell if necessary. Or try a non-magickal approach. If you are in any doubt at all, it's better not to cast the spell.

The Threefold Law

There is a very good reason for not sending out negative energy in your spells. It's called the Threefold Law. This second rule of magick states that whatever you send out, both magickally and mundanely, will return to you threefold. In some cultures this rule is known as karma, while other people like to call it the boomerang effect! Use whichever term you prefer, but remember that the basic principle remains the same. Everything you send out into the universe will come back to you with three times the force and three times the consequences. This is all well and good if your magick is positive, but if it is negative, there will be no avoiding the payback! An excellent reason, then, to ensure that your magick is positive in nature and harms none. Keep your witchcraft white and you won't go far wrong.

Spell only for what you truly need

The third rule of successful spellcasting is that you must actually need what you are casting for. If your magick is born of true need, it is far more likely to manifest, as you have a very personal investment in the magick and will be able to focus on it fully.

Timing

Timing your magick correctly is an intrinsic part of spellcasting. Moon phases, days of the week, and even times of day, all have an effect on your spells and rituals. The following information will help you to make the most of your magick. Although emergency spells should be cast as and when needed, regardless of the day or moon phase, other spells will benefit from being cast at a specific time, as this will help to harness the power of universal energies.

The lunar cycle

Each moon phase is suitable for specific types of magick.

New moon

This is when the moon first appears, as a thin sliver of light, in the sky. All spells for new ventures, new projects and new beginnings should be cast during this phase. The new moon is also good for spells concerning innocence and childhood and for general cleansings.

Waxing moon

This is the time when the moon grows from new to full. The light gradually increases, appearing to spread from right to left. All spells that work to bring something into your life should be performed during this phase. It is also particularly good for spells of growth and fertility.

Full moon

This phase, when all of the moon is visible, is the most powerful, and all spells can be cast effectively during it. You should also be aware that the night before and the night after the full moon are considered just as potent, effectively giving three whole nights of full moon power.

Waning moon

This is the time when the moon grows smaller in the sky, appearing to shrink from right to left. Witches use this phase to cast spells that remove unhelpful influences from their lives. These influences may range from poverty and bad habits to bad relationships and negative people. If you want to rid your life gently of something, then work at the time of the waning moon.

Dark moon

The moon is said to be dark when it isn't visible in the sky, usually two or three nights prior to the new moon. This is traditionally a time of rest, and the only types of magick worked during this phase are banishings (which pull someone or something away from you) and bindings (which freeze someone's or something's influence over you).

Blue moon

A blue moon occurs when there is more than one full moon within a single calendar month. This happens only once every few years, hence the expression 'once in a blue moon'. This is a time for setting long-term goals and for casting spells to manifest your dreams. Blue moon energy is rare and should never be wasted – you should always work some kind of goal-setting magick on this night.

Days of power

Each day of the week also lends different energies to your magickal work.

Monday

This is the day of the moon. It is good for spells that relate to your home, your pets, your family, feminine issues, psychic development and dreams.

Tuesday

Mars rules this day, making it perfect for any positive confrontation. Magick for business, work, getting your point across, courage and bravery should be worked on this day.

Wednesday

This day is ruled by Mercury, the winged messenger, so all spells for communication and creativity can be cast on this day.

Thursday

Thursday is ruled by Jupiter. It is a good day for money and prosperity spells, as well as holiday and travel magick.

Friday

This day belongs to Venus, so all spells for love, friends and socialising will be enhanced if performed on this day.

Saturday

Ruled by Saturn, this is a good day to do magickal work around paying off debts or calling in money owed to you. It's also good for releasing negative thought patterns and overcoming bad habits.

Sunday

This is the day of the sun. It is a great day for magick of self-love and masculine issues. It's fabulous for 'me time'!

Magickal colours

Different colours also have their own magickal symbolism and uses in spellcastings.

Black: Strong banishings, bindings, limitation, loss, confusion, defining boundaries

Blue: Healing, wisdom, knowledge, dreams

Brown: Neutrality, stability, strength, grace, decision-making, pets, family

Gold: Masculinity, sun power, daylight hours, riches, the God

Green: Finances, security, employment, career, fertility, luck

Grey: Cancellations, anger, greed, envy

Light blue: Calm, tranquillity, patience, understanding, good health

Orange: Adaptability, zest for life, energy, imagination

Pink: Honour, friendship, virtue, morality, success, contentment, self-love, chastity, romance

Purple: Power, mild banishings, ambition, inner strength, divination

Red: Love, valour, courage in adversity, allure, passion, sexual energy

Silver: Femininity, moon power, the night, the Goddess

White: Purity, innocence, cleansings, childhood, truth, protection

Yellow: Communication, creativity, attraction, examinations, tests

Magickal correspondences

When you cast a spell, it is important to use the tools, directions, colours and so on that are appropriate to – or correspond with – the purpose of the spell. Items, deities, gems and so forth that correspond in this way are known collectively as magickal correspondences. Part of the art of creating your own spells lies in matching together the appropriate correspondences with the correct moon phase and day of the week. Correspondences are grouped according to element.

Correspondences for Air

Angel: Raphael
Colours: Yellow, white, pale green
Crystals: Aventurine, jade, rose quartz
Direction: East
Season: Spring
Elemental: Sylph
Flowers: Snowdrop, daffodil, crocus, narcissus
Herbs and incenses: Sandalwood, dragon's blood, heather, meadowsweet, lemongrass, mint, clover, catnip, all seeds
Magickal hour: Dawn
Moon phase: Waxing
Oils: Daffodil, jasmine, heather
Trees: Birch, ash, apple, hazel

Correspondences for Fire

Angel: Michael
Colours: Gold, orange, bronze, red
Crystals: Citrine, carnelian, amber
Direction: South
Season: Summer
Elemental: Salamander
Flowers: Rose, foxglove, lilac, bluebell, sunflower
Herbs and incenses: Rose, violet, St John's wort, basil, dill, thyme, jasmine, vanilla
Magickal hour: Noon
Moon phase: Full
Oils: Rose, jasmine, violet, ylang ylang
Trees: Cedar, hawthorn, oak, willow

Correspondences for Water

Angel: Gabriel
Colours: Blue, turquoise, aqua, sea-green
Crystals: Turquoise, aquamarine, blue lace agate
Direction: West
Season: Autumn
Elemental: Undine
Flowers: Water lilies and aquatic plants, seaweeds
Herbs and incenses: Sandalwood, nutmeg, sage, mace, juniper
Magickal hour: Dusk
Moon phase: Waning
Oils: Oakmoss, patchouli, vetivert
Trees: Willow, rowan, blackthorn, sycamore

Correspondences for Earth

Angel: Uriel
Colours: Bark-green, brown, black, grey
Crystals: Tiger's eye, opal, quartz
Direction: North
Season: Winter
Elemental: Gnome
Flowers: All flowers and grasses
Herbs and incenses: Sage, bay, clove, basil, rosemary, bayberry
Magickal hour: Midnight
Moon phase: Dark moon
Oils: Frankincense, clove, cinnamon, pine
Trees: All trees and shrubs

Moving on ...

Throughout this chapter we have looked at the theory and magick of witchcraft and what it takes to cast a successful spell. As you can see, there is far more to spellcasting than meets the eye. In the next chapter we will be exploring the mechanics of faerie magick, and we will introduce ourselves to the Enchanted Realm!

Within the Hollow Hill

There is a place in a hollow hill
Where the sound of silver bugles trill.
There, in the bank that is covered all over
With the purple haze of summer clover
Sweet music plays the whole day long,
Filling the air with enchanted song.
Deep in the halls of the faerie hollow,
The Old Ones call and bid you to follow.
With enchantment and spell they lead you away
To become your hosts for a year and a day,
Learning the magick of glamour and spell,
Drinking the dew from the sacred well.
They teach you the little-known secrets of Earth
And help you to understand death and rebirth.
They teach you to sing, to heal and to dream;
They open your eyes to the seen and unseen.
Then they send you away with a protective charm
That your life may be happy and safe from all harm.

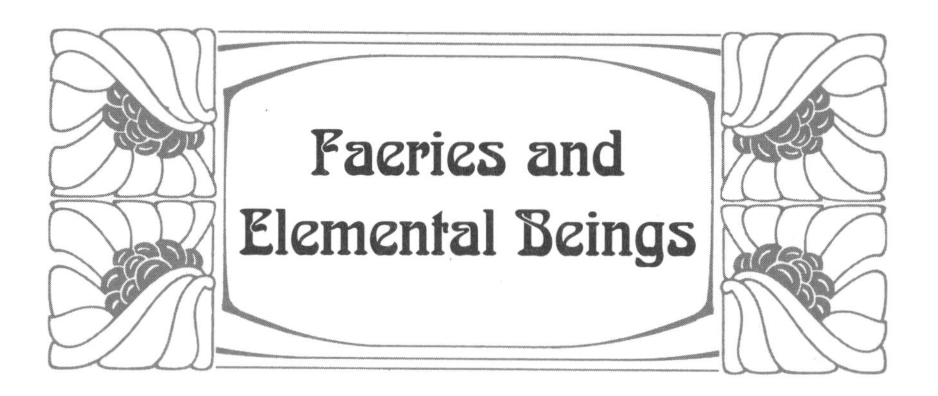

Faeries and Elemental Beings

When I was a small child, my bedroom was once redecorated with a beautiful faerie woodland wallpaper. One night, after I'd had a bad dream, my mother was sitting on my bed. She told me she'd picked the wallpaper because it was magick and that the faeries would protect me and watch over me as I slept. Then she began to make up bedtime stories about the various fairies that were dotted all over the walls. Such was my introduction to the Enchanted Realm.

Some of you reading this will no doubt have similar tales to tell from your own childhood. We invariably come across faeries during this time in our life, when everything is magickal and we see the world through innocent eyes. To many children it simply doesn't occur that faeries might not exist, so we live each day in perfect love and perfect trust, believing in the magick without a shadow of a doubt in our minds. As we get older, we are often laughed out of our faerie games. Feeling foolish, we turn away from the Enchanted Realm, allowing the portal to close behind us. Many people never find the portal again. Their childhood innocence and belief in magick and faeries is lost forever.

Some of us, however, choose to carry the magick forwards into adulthood, holding fast to the belief that there is more to this world than that which we see, and making every effort to keep the magick alive on a daily basis. We never forget the faerie realm of childhood and we somehow manage to retain a degree of innocence, while those around us become jaded by life and sceptical of magick. And we never stop looking for the portal we left behind so many years ago. Such people are the magickal practitioners and witches of today.

The fact that you are reading this book indicates that, on some level, you are seeking to find the magickal portal to the Enchanted Realm. Maybe you have an interest in faerie tale and folklore; maybe you want to discover more about the Enchanted Realm in general; maybe you just want to learn about magick and spellcasting. Whatever the reason behind your choice of reading material, you are responding to the voice of a faerie! And that means that you are one of the fortunate few for whom the magick never died!

What is a faerie?

In order for you to understand this book fully and make the most of the magickal concepts it contains, we must first clarify the difference between the terms 'fairy' and 'faerie'. The first of these refers to the creature known to most of us from children's storybooks. The faerie is usually female in form, with golden hair, glittering wings and a flower-petal dress. This image was largely popularised during the Victorian era, and while it is highly romanticised, there is nothing wrong with it. Pictures and statues of such creatures can be used to represent the true faeries – for example on an altar or in faerie spells. However, it should be pointed out that such faerie images are entirely imaginary.

True faeries are magickal elemental beings that preside over the natural world, ensuring that it ticks along exactly as it should, according to the due seasons of fertility and growth, decline and rest. They act as guardians of beauty spots and use their energy to repair damage and clean up pollution. Angels are one of the higher forms of elemental, holding power over the heavens, while faeries hold power over the earth. Both types of elemental can be called upon by witches and magickal practitioners to assist them in their spells and rituals. Witches and magickal practitioners can also work magick to help the elementals in their work of protecting the planet. Thus this is a magickal relationship of give and take.

A belief in faeries is common to cultures all over the world, and these beings are known by many names. As to who these elementals are and where they came from, there are lots of different ideas. Some say that faeries are the descendants of an old royal line who have left this world and now reside on a higher plane – the Irish Tuatha de Danaans are believed to be such a people. Others claim that faeries are ancient gods and goddesses who were forgotten long ago, and so in revenge they make mischief for human beings. Still others believe that faeries are a type of alien being. In the past, when Christianity was at its most fanatical, faeries were said to be fallen angels or demons sent by the devil.

Throughout history, faeries have been thought of as both good and bad, honoured and feared, but they have never been truly forgotten. From a very young age we are fascinated by them. Our imagination is captured by the idea of wood nymphs, dryads, elves and the other good spirits of the forest. The little people have danced through our earliest childhood dreams – and later proved to be the inspiration of musicians, writers, poets and artists alike.

To witches, faeries are the spirits of nature and the energy of the elements. We may choose to personify these energies and give them a human form, or the popular shape of a faerie, but we are always aware that the energies we are working with are real and very powerful. When a witch says that she believes in faeries, she is stating her acceptance of the universal life force of nature. Everything on our planet has its own energy, its own spark of divinity – every tree, every flower, every cloud, every blade of grass. This life energy is the elemental, the faerie. Believing in the existence of faeries is as natural and rational as believing in the existence of trees, for the one could not exist without the presence of the other.

As human beings, we feel the need to try to understand everything. We explore, we create, we research, we invent. And sometimes we resent the fact that we have come so far and yet still have much to learn. We want to know all there is to know, in a sense to achieve omnipotence. Some people dislike the fact that the earth should still hold mysteries and keep her secrets. So they tear to pieces, pull apart and rip to shreds that which they would know. They destroy all that they wish to discover – in short, they destroy the earth. Yet she keeps her secrets still! Witches understand that humankind are not meant to know all the secrets of the universe, and so we work with the elementals to try to repair some of the damage this arrogant human quest has caused.

Whereas in the past witchcraft was illegal and witches were persecuted, these days people are far more open-minded about and receptive to the idea of witchcraft and magick. Wicca is now one of the fastest-growing spiritualities in the Western world. At the same time, the Green movement has opened our eyes to the fact that the irresponsible behaviour of humankind is causing lasting damage to the environment. It should come as no surprise, then, that belief in faeries, including angels, is undergoing a revival, with more people than ever now attuning to and working with these elemental beings. The surprise is that the faeries still want to know us! Faeries are, after all, the spirits of nature, and we are the cause of so much destruction to the planet. Much of their energy is spent repairing the damage that we have recklessly caused to nature. If the faeries are shy to show their presence at first, who can blame them for their caution? However, if they are approached with patience and respect, faeries can become valuable magickal companions. And they have much to teach us if only we will learn.

Humankind's knowledge of the Enchanted Realm stems from a time when we were more in tune with the earth and our natural surroundings, when we were a part of the land, not above or separate from it. But as the woods and the wild places were cleared, the faeries retreated, and many of the portals to their realm were closed. From a distance they watched with sharp eyes, silently observing as forests were torn up and rivers and streams dammed. When humankind began to wake up to the mistakes that had damaged the environment and even jeopardised the long-term survival of the human race, then the elementals began to re-emerge.

Communicating with faeries takes time, patience and, above all, respect. They want to teach us how to love our planet, how to get joy from a daisy, freedom of spirit from a butterfly and cleansing from the blown spray of the ocean surf. Although they generally choose to keep a distance from the bright and noisy world of humanity, faeries are a significant part of our world. To invite them into your life is to invite joy.

The astral plane

The astral plane is a higher plane of existence. It is here that spirits, angels, familiars, guides, faeries and elemental beings reside. It is the realm of the unseen, which means that we cannot see the beings of this plane with our physical eyes, only with our mind's eye, or third eye, as it is also known. The third eye is located in the centre of the forehead, and is believed to be the seat of psychic abilities. In order to be better able to view the world through the third eye, some psychics choose to close their physical eyes as they work. In this way they are able to avoid distraction and open up the psychic channels.

The astral plane is also the place where dreams and visions take place. By using a technique known as dream incubation, some magickal practitioners are able to choose the kind of dreams they experience there. One practitioner may say to one another, 'I'll see you on the astral plane', meaning that they intend to meet up in their dreams. This is a powerful act of magick.

The astral plane plays a vital role in all types of magick. Indeed, effective spells cannot be cast without a close link with this higher realm. The Goddess and the God of witchcraft are attuned with via the astral plane, through the use of visualisation, dream work and meditation. In the Celtic belief system, this aspect of the astral plane is known as the Otherworld, and it is here that the gods, goddesses, heroes and heroines of legend are said to reside.

It is on the astral plane that the Enchanted Realm of the faeries is to be found. Here the nature spirits, angels, familiars and spirit guides dwell, watching over our world and protecting the natural resources of the earth. This part of the astral plane is thought to be the closest to the physical plane, so enabling elementals to pass back and forth from their world into ours. Where the two planes meet, magickal doorways, or portals, are created. Ley lines; a triad of oak, ash and thorn trees; ancient stone circles; and rings of mushrooms or toadstools are said to be such portals, and are often used as a focus for Otherworldly work by witches and magickal practitioners. Certain times of year also open up portals between our world and the astral world. Midsummer night's eve (on or around 21 June) has long been associated with faerie activity, while the witches sabbat of Samhain (or Halloween), on 31 October, allows spirits and ghosts to walk the earth once more.

Human beings are also a part of the astral plane. Each of us has an astral body, or spirit, which can pass through to the astral plane when we are asleep or in deep meditation. When we fall into a deep sleep, our astral body rises slightly, hovering above the physical body. This is a natural and harmless phenomenon, and it can give rise to pleasant dreams of flying or floating. This is usually followed by a falling sensation as the astral body returns to its physical host – causing the dreamer to wake up with a jump!

The imagination is the bridge that links our physical reality with the astral realm beyond, and a significant part of magick occurs within the practitioner's mind. By this I mean that the witch must have good visualisation skills to become adept at spellcasting. This is particularly important in faerie magick, as it is necessary to be able to visualise clearly the type of elemental you are calling on. A good imagination is a valuable asset to anyone keen on the magickal arts.

Thought forms

Witches and magickal practitioners sometimes send out a small part of their psychic energy in order to connect with the elementals, accomplish a particular goal or give protection. This energy is known as a thought form. The witch begins by creating an image in her mind, seeing the thought form in as much detail as possible. She then breathes life into her thought form, empowering it with her own energy, before giving it her magickal instructions.

The thought form is not a spirit or ghost, although some clairvoyant people may be able to see it in the same way they would see a spirit. In truth a thought form is an astral extension of the witch's psychic energy – or in some cases of the collective energy of an entire coven working together.

Thought forms are incredibly useful to the witch. It can be a great comfort to know that even while you are out at work, or at home sleeping, your thought form is out in the universe striving to manifest your magickal goal. In faerie magick, thought forms can be created to guard natural beauty spots or to keep away anyone who may have destructive plans for a local environment. Thought forms can also be created to act as a go-between, taking messages from the witch to the enchanted realm, as they exist on the cusp between our world and the astral plane, belonging wholly to neither one, yet being a part of both. We will be looking at various ways to use thought forms in faerie magick throughout this book, but for now let's begin with a simple exercise to create a particular thought form known as the Watcher.

To create a Watcher

When a thought form is given a human or animal shape and is used solely to protect someone or something, it is called a Watcher. Basically, the Watcher acts as an astral guardian, watching over you, your loved ones, your home and so on. If anyone with a negative intent comes within range of the Watcher's energy field, its presence will ensure that they feel a spooky sense of fear that makes them leave, pronto! Thus the Watcher is a useful magickal companion to have around. It is relatively easy to create, and you won't need any tools – only your imagination.

If you are creating a Watcher to protect a child, be aware that the child may pick up on its presence. Very young children are extremely perceptive and are naturally in tune with their own psychic abilities, so make your Watcher child-friendly, just in case! For instance, you might choose a traditional faerie godmother, an angel, an elf or their favourite superhero.

You will need: Nothing.
Moon phase: Any.

- Find a quiet place and sit comfortably on the floor, as if you were about to begin meditating. Close your eyes and breathe deeply a few times until you begin to relax.
- Once you feel calm and centred, start to imagine your Watcher before you. It's entirely up to you how you visualise this being, as he or she is a part of your own psyche. Your Watcher could be a ninja or a boxer; a Big Foot or a yeti. In the past I have used vampires, dragons and wolves as watchers, all to good effect. A popular form of Watcher is simply a dark shadowy figure, so if this is all you can see in your mind's eye, then that's fine too.
- Once you can clearly 'see' your chosen Watcher standing before you, lean forward slightly and breathe life into it by blowing into the visualised image three times. In this way you are breathing some of your own life essence into your magick. Then say the following charm out loud:

Watcher at the threshold, Watcher at the gate,
Protect me and mine from spite and hate.
Watcher at the threshold, Watcher at the gate,
Repel any foe and seal their fate.
So mote it be!

- Next give your Watcher detailed instructions as to who or what it is here to protect – for example, yourself, your car, your home, your child. If you have a particular fear of negative actions from a certain person, name this individual and instruct your Watcher to protect you from them, with harm to none.

- Visualise your Watcher fading out and know that your protection magick is now in place.
- Having created your Watcher, acknowledge the fact daily by chanting the charm above three times and visualising your Watcher at its post. This will help to keep the magick strong.

The elementals

Throughout this book we will be looking at different kinds of elementals and faerie beings. Collectively, these beings can be split into two categories: the major elementals and the minor elementals. The minor elementals are beings such as pixies, dryads, elves, wood nymphs and fire nymphs, while the major elemental groups are each associated with a particular element. These are as follows:

Gnomes

Gnomes are the elementals of Earth. They are associated with gardens, parks, hedgerows, meadows and groves. Their cousins, the dwarves, are linked with caverns and caves and the bowels of the earth.

Sylphs

The sylphs are the life force of the winds and the clouds. They work closely with the Water elementals to bring the rains and snows. They are the elementals of Air.

Salamanders

Salamanders are the small cousins of the dragons. They are the elementals of Fire and so are associated with all its manifestations, including lightning, electricity and sunlight.

Undines

'Undine' is the collective name for all Water elementals, be they sprites, mermaids or sirens. Undines are linked with oceans, rivers, streams, lakes, lochs, ponds and so on. They are also the bringers of rain, in which capacity they work closely with the sylphs.

Elementals for your birth sign

When you first begin to work faerie magick, you will need to establish a link with the Enchanted Realm and attune with the elementals you are invoking. Since you will have a natural affinity with the elemental of your birth sign, it makes sense to attune with the faeries of this element to begin with. Once you become more comfortable working faerie magick, you can start to work with the elementals of other birth signs, and the minor elementals as well. In this way you can work with the elemental most closely associated with your magickal goal. For instance, should you wish for a calm sea to ensure a safe and pleasant ferry crossing, you would address your wish to the undines of the ocean. To protect your home from accidental fire, you would work with the salamanders, and so on.

We will be looking in depth at each of the four major elemental groups over the next few chapters, but for know all you need to know is the element that your sun sign belongs to. The chart below will tell you this.

Sign	*Date*	*Element*	*Elemental*
Aquarius	21 Jan–18 Feb	Air	Sylph
Pisces	19 Feb–20 Mar	Water	Undine
Aries	21 Mar–20 Apr	Fire	Salamander
Taurus	21 Apr–21 May	Earth	Gnome
Gemini	22 May–21 Jun	Air	Sylph
Cancer	22 Jun–22 Jul	Water	Undine
Leo	23 Jul–23 Aug	Fire	Salamander
Virgo	24 Aug–22 Sep	Earth	Gnome
Libra	23 Sep–23 Oct	Air	Sylph
Scorpio	24 Oct–22 Nov	Water	Undine

Sagittarius	23 Nov–21 Dec	Fire	Salamander
Capricorn	22 Dec–20 Jan	Earth	Gnome

Birthdays on the cusp

If you were born on the cusp between two signs, i.e. on the first or last day of a sign, you are in a very fortunate position, as you will have a natural affinity with two types of elemental. The sign into which you were born will probably be a stronger influence over your personality, but you will also demonstrate aspects of your neighbouring sign too. In magickal terms, this means that you are doubly blessed and have the best of both worlds! For example, I was born on 22 November, which is the last day of Scorpio. This means that I have some Sagittarian traits and an affinity with the Fire element as well as my stronger Scorpio leanings and Water affinity.

The tools of faerie magick

As some of you are probably aware, witches use certain tools to perform rituals and cast spells. These are the tools of our trade, so to speak, and each has a purpose within the magickal arts. However, for faerie magick one or two of the standard witches' tools are inappropriate. This is because they are made from metal.

Folklore states that faeries are afraid of, or offended by, the magickal use of metals such as iron, steel and copper. Ever erring on the side of caution, witches take this into account when choosing their faerie magick tools. This means that the traditional witches cauldron and athame (ritual knife) should never be used in faerie magick. Instead, the tools of faerie magick are made from natural materials such as wood, clay, pottery and glass.

Wand

The faerie wand is a fallen twig, which should come from one of the triad of faerie trees, oak, ash and hawthorn. Alternatively, holly or willow can be used. The wand should reach from your inner elbow to the tip of your middle finger. It is used to direct energy.

Pentacle

The altar pentacle is a flat disk inscribed with a five-pointed star, or pentagram. This is a universal symbol of power, magick and witchcraft. The pentacle should be made from wood, clay or slate. Altar pentacles are available from New Age or occult shops. Alternatively, you can draw your own pentacle on an upturned terracotta plant saucer, or simply fashion a five-pointed star using fallen twigs and natural twine.

Besom

A besom is a witch's broom. It is invaluable in faerie magick, because it acts as a neon sign to the elementals saying, 'I'm a witch, talk to me!' It is used in cleansing and protection spells, and to sweep away negative energy, particularly from the area where magick is performed, known as the circle. In faerie magick the besom should be made from heather. Such brooms can be bought from New Age or occult shops.

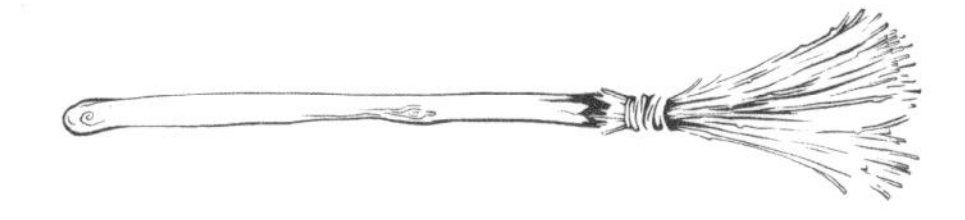

Brewing pot

This tool is a replacement for the iron cauldron. A simple casserole dish will do, particularly if it is of a natural colour or material. Ensure that your brewing pot is heatproof, as it will be used to brew potions, burn incenses and cast fire spells.

Chalice

This is a stemmed drinking vessel, used to hold the ritual wine or to administer potions. It should be made from glass, pottery or wood.

Faerie Grimoire

This is a version of the Book of Shadows, a witch's collection of spells, charms, rituals, poems, invocations and so on. If you already have a Book of Shadows, your Faerie Grimoire will form a chapter of this overall volume. If not – or if you prefer to have a separate volume – pick a book with a brown or green cover to symbolise the energies of nature and faerie magick.

Robes

Some witches choose to wear a special gown and cloak for magick, although this is not essential. If you would like to wear ritual robes for your faerie magick, choose ones in the colours of nature, such as earthy browns, foliage greens and berry reds. Feel free to mix and match.

The altar

A witch generally leaves all her magickal tools set out on a surface or table top, which then becomes a magickal altar. We will be exploring various altar set-ups in the following chapters, so choose the one you like best and feel an affinity with, unless you have the space to create several altars in your home. Alternatively, you may want to create different altars as you work with different elementals. For now, simply choose a surface in a quiet spot and place your ritual tools upon it. If you already have an altar set up, that's great; just make a few minor adjustments and add significant items as you work your way through this book.

The five-point faerie circle casting

Most magick is performed within a sacred space known as the circle. This is an area that encompasses the altar, the witch and all her magickal tools and items of spellcraft. Casting a circle is a visionary exercise, but in this instance we will be using pillar candles to mark out the space and create a visual boundary. This exercise should be repeated before every spell or ritual you perform.

You will need: 5 pillar candles, one of each of the following colours: silver or white, green, yellow, red, blue; five candle platters.

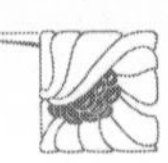

- Sit on the floor, facing the altar. Have all the candles, as well as matches or a lighter with you. Imagine that you are sitting in the centre of a clock face, and your altar is at 12 o'clock. Place the silver or white candle on the altar, light it and say:

  Akasha, spirit of all life, realm of the angels, the highest elementals, I bid you welcome.

- Place the green candle at two o'clock, light it and say:

  Earth, realm of the gnomes, I bid you welcome.

- Place the yellow candle at four o'clock, light it and say:

  Air, realm of the sylphs, I bid you welcome.

- Place the red candle at eight o'clock, light it and say:

  Fire, realm of the salamanders, I bid you welcome.

- Place the blue candle at 10 o'clock, light it and say:

  Water, realm of the undines, I bid you welcome.

- You should now be surrounded by the candles. Your faerie circle is cast and you can begin your spell. Try performing the simple one below.
- After performing your magick you should take the circle down. Do this by simply snuffing out the candles in reverse order of lighting, saying the name of the element and elemental, followed by the words:

  I release you.

Spell to open your heart to the faerie realm

Perform this spell in order to invite the faeries into your life.

You will need: nothing.

Moon phase: Any.

- Breathe deeply for a few moments and allow yourself to relax. Feel the power of magick all around you in the circle you have cast.
- Close your eyes and imagine that a golden, glittering bridge stretches out before you. In your mind's eye, notice how it sparkles and shines. Look across the bridge and see how it ends in a sea of swirling mists, beyond which lies the Enchanted Realm, where the elementals wait, ready to help you better your life.
- Concentrate on the image of the bridge for a few minutes, until it seems absolutely real to you and the path between yourself and the Enchanted Realm is strong.
- When you feel ready, visualise yourself taking a first step onto the bridge. In your mind's eye, keep walking until you reach the centre of the bridge, feeling the power and enchantment all around you as you go. Now say:

Hail to the powerful guardians of the elements, Earth, Air, Fire and Water. I am — (state your name) and I was born into the element of — (state the element you were born into). I come here in perfect love and perfect trust that I may make myself known to you. I recognise and acknowledge your mighty powers and I accept that power into my life. I ask for your aid, your wisdom, your assistance, your protection and, above all, I ask for your friendship. I open my heart and my mind to the Enchanted Realm and welcome the elementals into my life. Blessed be!

- Remain silent for a few moments, then visualise yourself turning and walking back across the bridge.
- Breathe deeply for a few moments, then open your eyes and know that you have sent a magickal message to the Enchanted Realm. You can now close your circle and go about your day.

Green Lady of the Forest

To see the Green Lady of foresty hues
Step into the woods and look for the clues:
A triad of trees, of oak, ash and thorn;
A shimmer of light as the world awaits dawn;
A collection of toadstools that push through the ground,
Forming a circle, perfectly round;
And there in the shade stands a moss-covered stone,
Which, on closer inspection resembles a throne.
Though winter lies heavy and the trees stand bare,
The fragrance of flowers pervades the cold air.
And we know she is coming when we hear her soft tread,
With her eyes feline-green and her lips rose-bud red.
For the snap of a twig is the sweep of her gown,
And the rustle of leaves is her hair hanging down.
Her mantle is woven from ivy and vine;
Her crown is the bramble and berry rose entwined;
Her slippers are silver, of cobweb made,
Lined with soft moss from a woodland glade;
Her dress is as fresh as the green leaves in spring,
For she is born of the earth and is part of all things.

Spirits of Earth

Deep within the hollow hills the spirits of Earth dwell. In every valley, grove and meadow, in every man-made park and garden, their energies can be attuned with and felt. As we discovered in the last chapter, the spirits of Earth are known as gnomes. The land is their domain, and their role is to maintain and care for the structure of the earth. It is no accident that gardens up and down the country boast collections of garden gnomes; by placing images of gnomes in our gardens we are unconsciously tapping into the gnomes' magickal powers and requesting their care and protection of our gardens.

Although these elementals are known in most parts of Britain as gnomes, in other places they go by other names. In Devon and Cornwall, for example, they are known as knockers and dwell in the tin mines, where it is considered to be bad luck to whistle underground as this offends the knockers and will cause a rock fall.

In Switzerland the Earth spirits are called the Kleinmanneken, which means 'little men', while in Germany they are known as Kobolds. In Russia they are called the polevik. Here, they dwell in cornfields, where their role is to protect – or hinder – the harvesters (depending on the tale).

Are you an Earth babe?

If you were born under one of the Earth signs, Taurus, Virgo and Capricorn, then you will already have a natural affinity with the gnomes and the spirits of Earth. This will probably be apparent in your life in some way, however subtly. Your home may be filled with house plants, or you may have created a beautiful garden and enjoy working here. Perhaps you enjoy cooking, using the gifts of the earth to create wholesome meals for your loved ones. Maybe you have a deep interest in the culinary, medicinal or magickal use of herbs. Perhaps the place where you live is itself connected with the spirits of Earth in some way. Do you live out in the countryside, or close to a woodland or meadow? Do you live in a mining village, or were you born into a mining family? If mining is in your background, you may already be very familiar with the Earth elementals, having grown up with bedtime tales about these Otherworldly cavern-dwellers.

It may be that your subconscious affinity with Earth elementals extends to your career and you work with the land in some way, as a farmer, geologist, ecologist or environmental scientist. Maybe you work in a garden centre or a herbal store, or even a New Age shop where natural magick is an everyday thing. Wherever you live, whatever you do for a living, if you were born into the element of Earth, the gnomes will have found some way to communicate with you, to guide you on your path and to make their magickal presence known. You may not have been aware of this until now, but in some way the element of Earth, your birth element, is strongly present within your life.

The magick of Earth

As some of you may know, each element is strongly associated with various types of magick and spellcasting. Earth power is close to all of us because the earth is our home. We therefore have a very special affinity with this element. (This is doubly so if you were born under the influence of an Earth sign.) The powers of Earth can be used for all spells of fertility, stability and growth. Earth energy also rules over finances, the home, career, savings, abundance and prosperity. All the spells in this chapter will focus on these areas.

The magickal colour of Earth is usually green, but brown is sometimes used too. Its direction is north, so place a green or brown candle at the 12 o'clock position on your altar to attune with Earth elementals and energies. The only exception to this rule is when you are casting a circle that has five points, such as the one on pages 37–8. In this case each point represents a point of the pentagram, with the top point being Akasha, the supreme spirit of all life. Thus all the elements are moved around slightly and Earth is found at the two o'clock position.

The season associated with Earth powers is winter, when Mother Earth takes her much-needed rest. The magickal faerie hour is midnight – this is the witching hour when all magick is doubly powerful. Earth energy is receptive, which means that it is a good element for pulling things towards you.

To attune with the elementals of Earth spend time in parks, gardens, caves, mines and meadows. Take part in an earthy sport such as rambling or horse riding. In the home, the kitchen is the room associated with Earth energies and elementals, so spend time here cooking, maybe preparing a dinner party for like-minded magickal friends. Study the magickal uses of herbs and begin to create your own Book of Shadows. Or get to grips with your garden and turn it into a magickal sacred space.

The gnomes and elementals of Earth are waiting for you to call upon them for assistance in your spells and rituals. To ensure you are working magick that is conducive to their energies, remember their key words: fertility, prosperity and abundance.

Creating an Earth altar

Most witches make use of altars. These are magickal places set up within our homes to enhance our personal space and to help us attune with specific energies. An altar is different from a shrine in that it is a space where magickal rituals take place, whereas a shrine is simply a place of reverence and honour. Creating an Earth altar within your home will invite the gnomes and other elementals of Earth into your life. It will help to bring the gifts of prosperity, abundance and growth into your home and may prevent your personal or professional life from stagnating.

You will need a sturdy surface for your Earth altar. A chest of drawers or a small table is ideal. Clean the surface well and drape it with a green or brown altar cloth, or paint it in one of these earthy colours. If your surface is made from solid wood, you might prefer to leave it uncovered. Two green or brown candles in appropriate holders should be placed towards the back of the altar as illuminator candles, and your magick faerie tools should be placed upon the altar too.

Now begin to decorate your altar by placing upon it items that suggest to you the powers of Earth and the gnomes. A healthy house plant is a good idea, as is a collection of pine cones and fallen leaves. You might like to make use of a garden gnome too. This will be a visual representation of the elemental your altar is dedicated to. If possible, get one of the garden gnomes designed to hold small garden tools. Remove the tools and fill the space with water, then use your gnome as an altar vase, arranging flowers where the tools should be.

In magick, rock salt is often used to represent the powers of Earth, so a small decorative container of this should be added to your altar too. If you are an Earth babe, you might like to include a representation of your birth sign. This could be a custom-made astrological ornament or simply a small statue of a bull for Taurus, a ram for Capricorn or a maiden for Virgo.

Holiday snaps can also be used as altar decorations. If you have a photograph of a particularly nice landscape, have it enlarged and place it in a wooden frame. Hang this above your Earth altar as a visual connection to the land. Alternatively, you could create your own landscape collage using magazine cuttings, postcards and finds from nature, such as pressed flowers and dried leaves.

Altars are always personal to the witch, so bear in mind that these are only suggestions. You may have specific ideas about what you want your Earth altar to look like, and that's fine. All magickal altars should serve to express the practitioner's individuality in some way. If you prefer a more discreet altar set-up, then arrange a few simple objects on your kitchen windowsill, remembering that the kitchen is linked with the powers of Earth. You might choose a green candle or tea-light in an appropriate holder, and a small statue of one of the Earth elementals – a gnome, dwarf, elf, pixie or nymph. In this way you are honouring and attuning with your chosen elemental while maintaining a degree of privacy regarding your magickal beliefs.

Some witches choose to set up an Earth altar outdoors in their garden. If you want to do this, you need to ensure that your garden is a very private place unless you want to be faced with awkward questions from nosey neighbours! If you do decide to go ahead with an outdoor altar, try using a trellis and climbing plants as a natural screen. Make sure the altar itself is heavy enough to resist strong winds – a small stone bench is ideal. Use lanterns rather than candles so that flames are enclosed and choose altar decorations that are weatherproof and designed for outdoor use. And do remember that a garden altar is usually much simpler than an indoor one.

To invoke the spirits of Earth

Before you begin working magick with the elementals of Earth, you will need to invoke them and welcome their energies into your life and your home.

You will need: Nothing.

Moon phase: Any.

- Go to your Earth altar and cast the circle as described on pages 37–8.
- Light the two illuminator candles at the back of the altar.
- Stand up and raise your arms high above your head, palms facing forwards. This is the position of invocation. Now invoke the spirits of Earth by saying:

I call on the mighty spirits of Earth,
Elementals of abundance, prosperity, fertility and birth.
I call your powers through time and space
And invoke your magick within this place.
So mote it be!

You are now ready to work any of the spells in this chapter.

Fertility magick

Fertility magick isn't just about conception and babies. It can also be used to bring a project or idea to birth, to increase the seeds of creativity and to enhance artistic talents. However, it must be said that women have long used the gifts of magick in order to aid the conception of a healthy child. In the past, women would have had to seek out a wise woman and ask for her help, but these days we can pick up a book like this one and work our own fertility charms. Such an idea shouldn't be scoffed at either, for although modern medicine can be effective in helping childless couples, conventional fertility treatment can also be an invasive and even humiliating experience. Magick is much gentler and may provide the kick-start your body needs to conceive. Fertility spells can be very effective, so if you're having problems starting a family, try a little magick in conjunction with your doctor's orders. One of my best friends made a fertility wreath (like the one in the spell below) and put May blossom beneath her bed after trying for over a year to conceive. As I write she is six months pregnant with twin girls!

Fertility wreath for conception

In this spell the red ribbon symbolises motherhood, the green ribbon symbolises fertility and the white ribbon symbolises children.

You will need: 9 pine cones; 9 acorns; some florists' wire; 1 red, 1 green and 1 white ribbon, each 1 metre (1 yard) long.

Moon phase: The next full moon after the sabbat of Ostara (21 March) or Beltain (1 May) or on either sabbat itself; alternatively, on any full moon.

- Knot the three ribbons together at one end and then plait them all the way down, as you do so visualising the conception of a healthy child.
- Using the florists' wire, attach the pine cones and acorns alternately, spacing them evenly down the length of the ribbon. This is somewhat tricky but do persevere.
- Once you have all the cones and acorns attached, tie both ends of the ribbon together to make a circular wreath.
- Place the wreath on your Earth altar and hold your hands over it, palms down. Now say:

I call on the gifts of the Earth elementals.

Spirits of Earth, empower this wreath and bless me with a healthy baby.

So mote it be!

- Leave the wreath in place for three days and nights and then place it over your bedpost or attach it to the headboard of your bed.

May blossom bed spell

You will need: Some spring water, a small statue or picture of a gnome, a boline or penknife.

Moon phase: Any – work on Beltain.

- Rise at dawn on the morning of Beltain (1 May). Go out for a walk and find a hawthorn tree, preferably with the dew still on it.
- Place your left hand on the tree and say:

Lady dryad of this tree,
I ask that three twigs you grant to me
For use in my spell of fertility.

- Wait for a moment and if all seems well, gently cut three small twigs of white May blossom, using the boline or penknife. If you feel uneasy in any way, leave the tree alone and find another.
- Once you have your twigs, take them home, place them beneath your bed in the shape of a triangle and sprinkle a little spring water on them. Place the statue of the gnome in the centre of this triangle and say:

It is a good mother I would be.
I ask for your gift of fertility.
This is my will. So mote it be!

- Leave the spell in place until conception occurs.

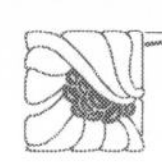

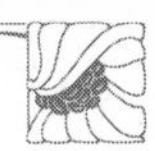

Faerie blessings for the bed spell

This is a very simple spell that calls the fertility blessings of the Earth elementals down into your bed, thus aiding conception in a magickal way.

You will need: A small stem of purple foxglove, your chalice, some rose water, a picture of an earthy type of faerie and a suitable wooden frame.

Moon phase: New to full.

- Place the picture of the faerie in the frame and leave it on your Earth altar to charge for three days and nights.
- Once the picture is charged, hang it on the wall above the head of your bed.
- Pour a little rose water into your chalice and turn the bedclothes back. Now dip the foxglove, which is a faerie flower, into the rose water and use it to flick and sprinkle the rose water all over the bed. As you do so, imagine yourself pregnant and chant the following charm nine times:

With faerie bloom and dew of rose
I bless the place of sweet repose.
Let love travel lightly, let conception be swift,
Let birthing be easy, pray grant me this gift.

- Put the foxglove under the mattress to increase the magick and pour the remaining rose water into the garden.

A general fertility charm

This spell can be used to work for any form of growth and fruition, for example a promotion at work, a healthy savings account or a creative project.

You will need: A small green pouch, some fresh rainwater, a few poppy seeds, a silver faerie charm, an aventurine crystal, a silver pentacle charm, a green pen, a slip of paper, a green ribbon.
Moon phase: Waxing.

- Place all the spell items on your altar pentacle to charge for 24 hours.
- Go back to your altar and cast the circle as described on pages 37–8.
- Light the illuminator candles and then write your magickal goal on the slip of paper using the green pen. Then roll the spell paper up and place it into the pouch, as you do so saying:

Herein lies the purpose of my spell.

- Add the faerie charm to the pouch, as you do so saying:

I invoke the magick of the faerie realm, of the elementals and spirits of Earth.

- Add the aventurine crystal, as you do so saying:

I fertilise this goal with the powers of Earth.

- Add the poppy seeds, as you do so saying:

I sow the seeds of my goal and realise my dreams.

- Add the silver pentacle charm, as you do so saying:

I empower my goal with the gift of magick.

- Tie the neck of the pouch with the green ribbon, as you do so saying:

I bind this goal with the gift of success.

- Sprinkle the whole pouch with the rainwater, as you do so saying:

I bless this goal with the gift of the gods. This spell is done. So mote it be!

- Keep the spell pouch with you at all times until the goal manifests.

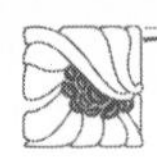

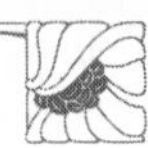

Leaf letters spell

This is a quick and easy spell that you can use at any time for any goal. It is a kind of petition magick, which means that your request is written down and then released into the universe in some way. In this case the spell is released in a woodland, park or garden, close to the elementals and their natural energies.

You will need: A gold pen, a hole punch, a green ribbon, a small bun or cake

Moon phase: Any.

- ◆ Go out and find a large leaf – sycamore leaves are great for this spell.
- ◆ Take the leaf to your Earth altar and ask for the blessings of the gnomes.
- ◆ Using the gold pen, write your goal or magickal request on the back of the leaf. You may need to narrow your goal down to key words or a short sentence in order to fit it on the back of the leaf.
- ◆ Hold the leaf to your heart, close your eyes and visualise an Earth spirit. How you see this elemental is your choice but try to get a clear image in your mind. When you have the image say:

Spirit of Earth, elemental friend,
I call you here your powers to lend.
This leaf holds a message for you and your kind;
Please manifest my dreams and success let me find.
So mote it be!

- ◆ Open your eyes and, using the hole punch, punch a hole through the leaf near to the stalk. Thread the green ribbon through the hole.
- ◆ Take the leaf letter out to a woodland and tie it to a tree to release the magick of the spell. Place the bun or cake at the foot of the tree as an offering and thanks.

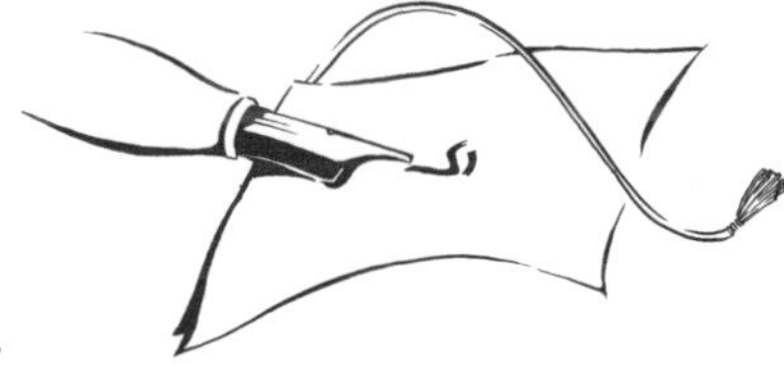

Prosperity and abundance magick

The world is a naturally abundant place, and there is no need for struggle and hardship. One of the first things you should do before performing any abundance magick, however, is get to grips with any debts by making prompt and regular payments. Also curb any unnecessary spending. I'm not saying that you should never treat yourself, but be realistic about how much income you have and buy treats for yourself only when you can afford to do so without getting into debt. While the following spells will certainly help to bring prosperity and abundance to your door, they won't pay off your mortgage or the finance on your car! To reap the best results be realistic in your prosperity magick goals, asking for just a little more than you need and no more.

To invite the Abundance Faerie into your life

On pages 31–3 we looked at the concept of thought forms and how to create them. Here we will be creating a special thought form to attract the gifts of prosperity and abundance. I call her the Abundance Faerie, but you might prefer a different name. I usually visualise this thought form as a beautiful maiden, dressed in shades of pale green and gold. She carries a magickal cornucopia under her arm, from which she can give me all the abundance and prosperity I need. If you feel comfortable with this image, then by all means use it, but if not, feel free to create your own vision.

You can ask your Abundance Faerie for financial help, such as a pay rise at work, the approval of a mortgage, or money to pay a specific bill. Alternatively, you might like to ask her to help ensure the financial success of a new business venture or to guide you towards the right investments. Your wish should manifest within three months. A larger goal, such as a mortgage, for example, will take longer to manifest.

You will need: Nothing.
Moon phase: Any.

- Cast the circle as described on pages 37–8 and then follow the instructions for creating the Watcher on pages 31–3, altering your visualisation to see instead the Abundance Faerie.
- Once you have breathed life into your Abundance Faerie thought form, speak the following incantation in order to activate her:

Faerie of prosperity, of riches and wealth,
Fill my financial life with good health!
Let me know plenty; I'll give as I take.
Abundance for all is a wish I would make!

- Now ask your Abundance Faerie for any particular help with abundance that you require. Imagine her reaching into her magickal cornucopia and handing you your wish. Then see her fade out in a gleam of green light.
- As always when working prosperity magick, end your spell with the words:

I work this magick with harm to none.

This will ensure that your financial gain doesn't come from a negative source.

- Now that you have created your Abundance Faerie, you can call on her at any time by repeating the incantation above and making your request.

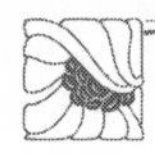

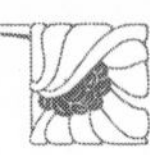

The Gnome of Plenty

For this little spell you will need a small garden gnome. If he is dressed in green, then so much the better, as this is the colour of prosperity, abundance and Earth magick. Remember that this statue is merely a representation of the natural energies you are calling on. Its main purpose is to help you focus your mind and provide a visual link with the Earth elementals.

You will need: A garden gnome statue, some patchouli oil, a small paintbrush, a green pen, a slip of paper, some sticky tape.

Moon phase: New to full.

- Take the gnome to your Earth altar. Cast the circle as described on pages 37–8 and light the illuminator candles.
- Using the paintbrush, carefully anoint the gnome with the patchouli oil, giving him an even covering. Patchouli has long been used by witches for its prosperity-drawing powers.
- Using the green pen, write the following spell on the slip of paper:

By the powers of Earth energy,
I ask the elementals to bring me plenty.

- Fold the spell paper and tape it securely to the underside of the gnome.
- Take down the circle, as described on page 38, blow out the altar candles and then stand the gnome on your front doorstep or close to the main entrance to your home to attract abundance and plenty in through the door.

Give something back ...

Elemental magick works both ways, which means that while it is perfectly acceptable to request faerie assistance with your spells for life improvement, you must be prepared to give a little bit back in turn. This needn't be a huge undertaking. An increased awareness of environmental issues would be a good start, accompanied by changes in your behaviour such as introducing a home recycling plan for your household and where possible buying only organic and free range foods.

You might also try meditating on a green candle and visualising fresh green fields, lush meadows and healthy crops free from chemicals. This will help to send your magickal energies out to the spirits of Earth, where they will put them to good use.

A more immediate way to help the gnomes and spirits of Earth is to invest in a small hedgehog home and place it in a secluded spot in your garden. In some folklore traditions, the hedgehog is a faerie in disguise! So make hedgehogs welcome and invite them to set up home in your magickal garden. This will be a positive sign that you are offering your assistance to the spirits of Earth.

The Four Winds

Boreas comes from the northern plain,
His icy breath making snow from rain.
His wintry cloak of silver and white
Is magickally trimmed with northern light.
While Eurus, his brother, comes of the east,
Bathing the sky in a golden feast.
He trails in the wake of Aurora, the dawn,
And brings the soft dewdrops that herald the morn.
From the south comes Notus, whose breath is so warm,
Stirring the fields of ripening corn.
He murmurs through meadows and whispers through wheat
And brings welcome freshness to all that he meets.
Next, gentle Zephyrus comes out of the west,
Bringing the rain, the fog and the mist.
Clothing the world in a dull dampened shroud,
His breath is a drizzle and his cloak the grey cloud.
We welcome each wind as he passes close by,
Changing the landscape and painting the sky.
For each has a purpose and each knows his place,
And we smile as we watch the clouds drift and race.

Spirits of Air

The spirits of Air are known as sylphs. They govern every strong wind and gale, every soft breeze, and are present in every cloud formation. At their most negative the sylphs can produce a destructive tornado, while in their gentler moods, they bring the cooling breeze on a hot summer's day.

The sylphs are said to be the guardians of the higher self during astral travel. They can assist in matters of meditation and journeying, astral projection and making contact with the spirit world. They are the keepers of inspiration and can aid creativity. In this sense they are often called the muses, after the nine muses of Greek mythology.

Sylphs go by many names. The sixteenth-century alchemist Paracelsus sometimes referred to them as sylvestres. Paracelsus is responsible for much of our modern view of the magickal elementals, even down to the names that modern witches and magickal practitioners give to the four main elemental groups – gnomes, sylphs, salamanders and undines – which are those that Paracelsus himself chose.

In Hindu mythology the sylphs are called the asparas, or sky dancers. In Switzerland the Fantine are the weather faeries, while in the Orkney Islands Teran is the storm faerie who brings winter in. Celtic banshees are also a form of sylph, and we will be looking at these elementals shortly.

Are you an Air babe?

If you were born under one of the Air signs, Gemini, Libra and Aquarius, you will probably find it difficult to keep your feet on the ground! This is largely due to your natural affinity with the Air elementals. You may find that you are rarely in one place for very long and feel the need to be constantly on the go. You may even be accused by some of being flighty! As an Air sign – it is not in your nature to remain grounded!

The elementals of Air will speak to you on a subconscious level, reminding you of your need for flight and movement. This could be apparent in may ways. Perhaps you love to travel, liking nothing better than to see new places and take to the skies in a plane. You might also enjoy fairground rides – the higher and faster the better, as it is unlikely that you have a great fear of heights. You love to feel the wind in your hair or to lie back and watch the clouds race by.

You may enjoy extreme sports such as mountain climbing, hang-gliding, paragliding or even skydiving. If you've always secretly longed to jump from a plane in a parachute or learn how to fly a jet, this is your elemental speaking to you. This desire could even urge you into a career with a mountain rescue team or the air force.

Perhaps, though, the sylphs speak to you in a gentler way, inspiring you to learn to play a musical instrument or belt out a song. These are the beings of music and creativity, after all. Do you feel an affinity with birds? Maybe you have an aviary or are involved in bird protection. In some way, in some form, the elementals of Air have a strong presence within your life, and the sylphs are communicating with you on a daily basis.

The magick of Air

The element of Air is essential for survival. Without air our entire world and all in it would die, yet we rarely stop to think about the pollution we are causing as we start up our cars in the morning. We take it for granted that there will always be enough oxygen for us to breathe, yet we immediately notice the purity of the atmosphere when we leave the city and go out into the countryside or up into a mountainous region. To work with the sylphs you will need to develop a little forethought with regard to pollution. This may mean walking the kids to school instead of taking them in the car, or buying products that are environmentally friendly.

The powers of Air are used in spells for inspiration, creativity, communication, intelligence, tests and examinations, vocal and musical talents, poetry and the arts. The sylphs will help you to write and perform a speech or presentation. They will urge you in your ambitions, be this to write a book; to take up art; to become a poet, dancer or actor; or to obtain a recording contract. It is the sylphs that prompt you to stop dreaming of your goals and start actively pursuing them. And they can be called upon to help bring success your way. Of course, you will still have to work hard and develop your talent; magick won't do all the work for you, but it can give you an edge over the competition! The sylphs will make sure that you are in the right place at the right time, talking to the right people. As the elementals of communication, they help to build bridges between people, and so working with their energies can help to move your life forward and make your personal goals more easily attainable.

In witchcraft the colour used to represent Air is yellow. The direction of Air is east, dawn is its magickal faerie hour and spring its season. Air is a projective energy and as such it can be used in two ways: to remove negative aspects from your life and to project yourself and your talents forward in the world. People who work in the performing or creative arts often feel an affinity with this element and its power. The sylphs are also a very important elemental for those people who work from home, and if you have a library, study, office or studio within your house or flat, then this part of the house is ruled by the spirits of Air.

To attune with the Air spirits go out for a walk on a windy day, climb to the top of a hill and feel the wind in your hair. Or laze around the garden on a warm summer's day and observe the various formations the clouds make. Collect fallen feathers or teach yourself the art of augury, which is divination by bird flight. Fill your life with music, song and dance, for these are the gifts of the sylphs. To ensure that you are working magick that is conducive to their energies, remember their key words: creativity, communication, grace and talent.

Creating an Air altar

If possible, place your Air altar in an eastern position within your home. Alternatively, you could set it up in an area of the house that is naturally connected to the element of Air, for example the study or home office. As a result you will probably find that work goes more smoothly and you become more productive as the elementals of Air lend their powerful energies to your personal efforts.

Cover your chosen surface with a yellow cloth and place two yellow candles in appropriate holders towards the back of the altar as illuminators. Now decorate the altar to represent the elementals

it is dedicated to. Fill a vase with naturally shed feathers or tie pretty ribbons to a small desk fan and switch this on when you are working at the altar. Buy a feather boa to trim the edge of your altar surface. Place a mask made from feathers on your altar, too. This is great for adding an air of mystery to your rituals and for seduction magick!

Add statues of traditional fairies to lend a feeling of enchantment, or perhaps figures of birds if you prefer. Any wispy, ethereal-looking maiden would be appropriate for an air altar, as would small statues of graceful dancers, such as ballerinas. Add a set of pan pipes or a flute, or maybe even a small harp or lute. Listen to harp music while meditating on the sylphs and invest in a lovely incense burner. In magick, incense is used to connect with the powers of Air, so regular incense burning is an intrinsic part of sylph magick. If you are an Air babe, add an ornament to represent your birth sign – a small water urn could be used for Aquarius, a miniature set of scales for Libra, and a figure or picture of twins for Gemini.

Finally, hang a picture of fluffy white clouds above your altar as a visual link with the elementals of Air.

To invoke the spirits of Air

Before you begin working with the elementals of Air you will need to invoke them and make their energies welcome in your life and your home.

You will need: Nothing.

Moon phase: Any.

- Go to your Air altar and cast the circle as described on pages 37–8.
- Light the two illuminator candles at the back of the altar.
- Stand up tall and raise your arms high above your head, palms facing forwards, in the position of invocation and say:

I call on the mighty spirits of Air,
Elementals of inspiration, creativity, ambition and communication.

I call your powers through time and space
And invoke your magick within this place.
So mote it be!

The banshee

The banshee, or *bean sidhe,* is a sylph-like figure of Celtic origin. Her name means 'woman of the faeries', and traditionally she attaches herself to a particular clan. She is usually depicted as a beautiful maiden in a tattered grey or white dress and a white cloak that streams out behind her as she flies through the air. She has very long hair, usually red but in some traditions white-blond. She sings in a high-pitched wail, known as keening, and her appearance foretells a disaster or tragedy.

In some tales the banshee is seen sitting in the bare branches of a winter tree, combing out her long locks by the light of the moon. Her expression is always sad or distraught, her eyes red and swollen from weeping. To hear the keening of a banshee is said to be bad luck, while to actually see one is a warning, sometimes of death. Although this elemental doesn't fit the stereotypical faerie image, she is none the less a member of the fey, as the true meaning of her name indicates. As she floats through the air unaided, she is linked with the sylphs and is a spirit of Air. In some legends, she is accompanied by magickal singing birds, usually three in number.

To create a banshee thought form

Although an actual banshee sighting would probably be unpleasant to say the least, there is a positive way to use the banshee's energies in magick. By creating your own personal banshee thought form, you can ensure that you are forewarned of any forthcoming disaster. You will then be able to take steps to alter your present course of action and so avoid the problem.

- Go to your altar, light the illuminator candles and cast the circle as described on pages 37–8.

- Follow the instructions for creating the Watcher thought form on pages 31–3, altering your visualisation to see instead a beautiful red-headed banshee with wild eyes, pale skin and ruby lips. This is your personal banshee of warning. Her role is to guide you away from any avoidable disaster, trouble or tragedy. She is not meant to frighten you in any way but to protect and guide you and provide a clear warning when you are on the wrong path.
- Once you can see your banshee clearly and have breathed life into her, say the following incantation to activate her powers:

Banshee with your wailing song,
Tell me when I'm going wrong.
If a mistake I'm about to make,
Warn me and another path I'll take.
Alert me with your keening voice
And guide me to a different choice.

- See your banshee slowly fade away.
- Now that you have activated this thought form of warning, pay attention! If your banshee makes a sudden appearance in your dreams, or in your mind's eye at any time, take heed of her warning and alter your actions accordingly.

Feathers of fortune divination

Divination is the art of fortune-telling. There are many ways to practise it and many tools that can be used. This spell makes use of a simple method in which coloured feathers are the means of interpretation.

If at all possible, collect your feathers from nature, picking up those that have been naturally shed and match the colour you need as closely as possible. Alternatively, buy them from an art supplies store, but do ensure that they are cruelty-free.

You will need: A small black pouch; your altar pentacle; 6 feathers, one in each of the following colours: black, white, blue, red, brown, green; a seagull's feather.

Moon phase: full.

- Place your seven feathers in the pouch and put the pouch on your altar pentacle to charge for three days and nights. The feathers are then ready to be used as a divination tool.
- Holding the pouch of feathers in your hand, close your eyes and concentrate on the question you wish to ask. Continue focusing on the question for a few minutes, then carefully pull one of the feathers from the pouch. Use the interpretations below to find your answer, based on the feather you selected.

  Black feather: You are on a magickal path and are guided by the Morrigan. A good sign.

  Seagull feather: Seagulls are considered to be bad omens and bad luck. This is a negative answer, so alter your course.

  White feather: You are protected by angels. Everything is happening for your highest good. A very positive answer.

  Blue feather: You have the ability to attain new heights, so reach for the sky!

  Red feather: You can rise from misfortune like a phoenix from the flames! Also denotes love and passion.

  Brown feather: Take no immediate action, but try to remain grounded for a while.

  Green feather: A sign of comfort and security. Take time to build your nest and create a nest egg.

Seduction dance

The sylphs are all about movement, balance and grace, so a great way to draw on their powers is to dance. Dance is a magickal spell in its own right – and it will make you feel good too. Your body becomes the tool; the music is the inspiration. You don't need to be a classical ballerina or a queen of the fox trot either; we all have a natural sense of balance and grace or we wouldn't be able to walk upright! Dancing is also a fabulous way to improve your relationship with your body, and it can put an added zing in your relationship if you're brave enough to dance for your man.

First set the scene. Push the furniture back out of the way and then dim the lights. Soft lighting is flattering and it will help you to relax and feel comfortable with yourself. Next call on the sylphs and ask for their gifts of music, movement and grace. You can do this out loud or in your head. Light a few candles if you wish, but make sure they are out of the way and won't be knocked over once you start jumping to the beat! A glass of wine will help you to release your inhibitions, and a soothing oil in an oil burner will create an atmosphere of peace and calm.

If you are dancing for your man, place a chair in the middle of the room. If you're dancing alone, perhaps to raise power for a spell you want to perform afterwards, keep the area free of clutter. Now select your music. This should be quite slow but with a beat that you can move to. Choose something sexy and seductive and which inspires graceful movement. Wear something both sexy and comfortable that won't restrict your movement in any way. Unless you are used to high stiletto heels, dance barefoot – that way you won't be in danger of a twisted ankle! Finally, try putting on a feather mask and wearing a feather boa to invoke the power of the spirits of Air. Now start to dance.

You will soon feel like the sexiest of sylphs and your man will realise that there's more to you than meets the eye! For an added boost, work the following spell beforehand.

A spell for sylph-like grace

You will need: Your imagination.
Moon phase: Any.

- Go to your Air altar and light the illuminator candles. Sit for a while and bring to mind the image of a beautiful sylph.
- Meditate on this image for a while and then say the following incantation three times:

A sweet seductress I would be
To keep my man true to me.
I call the sylphs through time and space

To bless me with their gift of grace.
So mote it be!

- Stay at the altar for a few moments, focusing on the energies you have called. Then blow out the candles and move through your day with a new-found grace.

The four winds

In Greek mythology the spirits of the four winds are male. Their names are Boreas (the north wind), Eurus (the east wind), Notus (the south wind) and Zephyrus (the west wind). Each wind ushers in a particular type of weather and is linked with one of the four seasons. This means that they are the perfect allies when it comes to casting spells to determine the weather – a technique known as weather witching. They can also be called upon for magickal help in particular areas.

Boreas (north): Brings ice, snow, sleet and gales. He brings winter in and presides over spells of rest, security, completion and banishings. He can help to 'freeze' a situation.

Eurus (east): Brings the dewdrops at dawn, light showers and gentle rain. He brings in the season of spring and presides over spells for new beginnings, fertility, abundance and growth. He can help with magick for youth and beauty.

Notus (south): Brings the warm winds and nurturing rains. He brings in the season of summer and presides over spells for love,

passion, lust, seduction and prosperity. He can assist with magick for fidelity and will help you to put new heat into an old relationship.

Zephyrus (west): Brings hard, driving rains, thick fogs and swirling mists. He brings in the season of autumn and presides over spells for cleansing, purification, healing, release, dreams and psychic abilities. He can help you to see through the fog of a situation or to veil a situation from prying eyes.

Spell of the four winds

This is a very simple spell to perform.

You will need: A wind instrument such as a flute or recorder (optional), a compass (optional).
Moon phase: Any.

- Use the list above to determine which of the wind spirits you wish to call up.
- Use the compass, if necessary, to determine your wind spirit's direction, then, facing that direction, simply whistle or play a tune. This is called whistling in the wind. As you whistle in your chosen spirit, focus your mind on your magickal goal and use your visualisation skills to ensure the best results from your wind spells.

Spell for communication

If you wish to hear from old friends or would like better communication with a loved one, call on the powers of the sylphs for assistance.

You will need: A citrine crystal, your altar pentacle, a faerie statue or picture, your wand, a slip of yellow paper, a yellow or gold pen.
Moon phase: Waxing.

- Go to your Air altar, light the illuminator candles and cast the faerie circle as described on pages 37–8.
- Using the yellow or gold pen, write your communication wish on the slip of yellow paper.

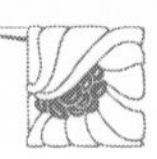

- Place the paper on the centre of your altar pentacle and put the citrine crystal on top. This crystal has long been used by witches as a channel for communication. Place the faerie statue just behind the pentacle.
- Take up your wand and move it in a clockwise direction three times around the crystal. As you do so say:

Spirits of Air, powers that be,
Assist my magick. So mote it be!

- Now leave the spell in place for a full lunar cycle, during which your communications should see an improvement.

A spell to call your muse

As the keepers of inspiration and creativity, the sylphs and spirits of Air are often called muses. We all have a muse, and we can call on her at any time by doing this spell.

You will need: A statue or picture of a muse-like figure, a candle and suitable holder.
Moon phase: Any – perform whenever you need inspiration.

- Place the candles and representation of your muse on your desk or in your work space and light the candle.
- Call your muse by repeating the following charm three times:

I call my muse through time and space
To settle here within this place.

- Wait until a sense of calm descends upon you. This is the arrival of your muse and the inspiration you have called. Now settle down to your work.
- Remember to thank the muse and blow out the candle when your work is complete.
- Repeat this spell each time you begin to work on a creative project.

A spell to encourage creativity

To enhance this spell, perform it in conjunction with the one above.

You will need: An oil burner fashioned to look like a faerie, your favourite oil.

Moon phase: Any.

- Hold your hands, palms down, over the oil burner and empower it by chanting the following charm:

Faerie of creativity,
I call your powers here to me.
Fill my mind with visions strong;
Let me work the whole day long.
Help me to perfect my art;
Here is where my dreams will start.
Let the words/notes/images comes swift and true.
Sacred being, inspire me do!

- Use the burner to burn the oil as you work. Each time you light the burner, repeat the charm once more.

Give something back ...

When working with the spirits of Air to improve your life, it is important that you give a little back. This means developing an awareness of air pollution and doing your part to eliminate it. Meditating on the flame of a white candle and visualising a clean, clear atmosphere, free from pollution, is a positive start. This will help to send your magickal energy out to the sylphs, who will put it to good use.

Another, more practical, way in which you can give something back to the Air spirits is to feed the birds. Do this on a regular basis, most especially through the winter months. You could set up a bird table or hang bird treats from the trees and shrubs in your garden. A nice touch is to invest in a hanging bird feeding bowl that has a ceramic faerie sitting on one side. Fill this with nuts and seeds and hang it in your garden for the local birds. This will act as a clear indication that you are offering your assistance to the spirits of Air.

Salamander

Tiny dragon of red-hot flame,
Of electric blue and embers deep,
Salamander is your name.
Powers of Fire are those you keep;
Passion and protection are your charms.
As we summon you with candles bright,
Power to transform and power to harm,
We are careful not to abuse your light,
Love and lust and heartfelt desire.
All this and more salamanders teach,
Smouldering temper, feisty spitfire,
For those born under a Fire sign's reach!
And deep within your sacred glow,
For those who do not fear the burn,
True love awaits for those who know
That give and take have an equal turn.

Spirits of Fire

Fire! It has the ability to heat and to nurture life and it has the power to disfigure and kill. It is the trickster of the elements and, like all tricksters, it must be treated with the utmost respect and its power invoked with caution. Fire spells should always be approached with a large dose of common sense. When working fire rituals, short sleeves are advisable – this is not a time for sweeping *Lord of the Rings* style gowns or flowing ritual robes. Long hair should always be tied back in order to avoid an impromptu witch burning! And always have a fire extinguisher or a large bucket of water handy, just in case!

The spirits of Fire are known as the salamanders. No fire, flame or form of heat exists without their presence, and so they are an intrinsic part of our everyday lives. They are present in all forms of electricity, so every time you use the straightening irons or curling tongs on your hair, or lie on a sunbed, you are utilising their power. Without the energy of these elementals you couldn't boil a kettle, heat the house, watch TV or surf the internet.

The salamanders are also present in more obvious ways, such as the flame of a ritual candle, the heat of the sun, a bolt of lightning and, of course, the bonfires and firework displays that take place all over the UK on the 5th of November.

In magickal terms, salamanders are cousins of the dragons, though they are somewhat smaller. They are generally visualised as tiny dragons of flame-like hues – reds, golds and deep oranges. Electrical salamanders are seen as white, blue and violet. Lots of magickal people already feel a deep affinity with the salamanders, because most spells and rituals make use of their power in the form of candles. In their more negative aspect, salamanders are responsible for lightning storms, explosions, accidental fire and volcanic eruptions. Their main roles in magick are protection and purging unwanted influences from our lives.

Spirits of Fire are also associated with romantic relationships. In this sense I prefer to visualise them as flaming fire nymphs, but this is a personal choice. While it is the undines of Water who preside over the area of love and enchantment, the spirits of Fire are associated with the heat of lust and passion and that first initial spark you feel when you are attracted to someone. Both elemental groups can assist you in developing a positive body image and learning the art of seduction. We will be looking at this a little later.

Will o' the Wisp

The Will o' the Wisp is an ethereal light seen flickering over swamps and marshland. This embodiment of fire is caused by the various gases rising from the marsh and igniting. Although this is an entirely natural phenomenon, it has given rise to many legends and much folk belief and superstition.

This form of Fire spirit has many names. It is called William with the Little Flame and Will o' the Wykes in England. In Irish folklore it is known as the water sheerie, and in Scotland it is called the teine sith, or fire faerie. Faerie lanterns, earth light, elf light and elf fire are all other names for the Will o' the Wisp.

In its darker aspect the Will o' the Wisp is often called a corpse candle. In this respect it is said to be an omen of death, either of the person who sees it or perhaps of someone they know. As Will o' the Wisps hover and dance over dangerous marsh- and bogland, it is never wise to follow these little flames. They should be observed from a safe distance!

Are you a Fire babe?

If you were born under one of the Fire signs, Aries, Leo and Sagittarius, you will already have a strong affinity with the spirits of Fire. You are probably passionate in all that you do, though you could be accused of being unpredictable and fiery-tempered! You are likely to be a true sun queen, liking nothing better than exotic holiday destinations where you can lie on the beach all day. When there's no sun shining, you take to the sunbed instead. Love and passion are always high on your agenda, and you are ambitious, driving towards your ultimate career goals.

The salamanders will speak to you on a subconscious level, urging you to fill your home with scented candles, invest in a sunbed, live or work abroad in a hot country, or cosy up next to a roaring log fire. People born into the element of Fire are usually very productive. They are good leaders and like to take charge. They also enjoy being the centre of attention! As a Fire babe you have the ability to shine in your own right. This could lead you to a career in the performing arts or in a field where verbal presentations and performance are a part of your day. You tend to choose jobs and careers where you or your work is in some way on display. Again, this is the strong influence of the salamanders giving you a burning desire to be noticed and acknowledged!

The magick of Fire

Fire magick is an intrinsic part of nearly all spellcastings and rituals. The power of Fire is present throughout the spells of this book in the form of the illuminator candles on the altar and the five pillar candles that mark out the boundary of the magick circle.

The colour of fire is, obviously, red, though shades of orange and gold are also used to represent this element. Its direction is south,

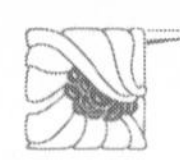

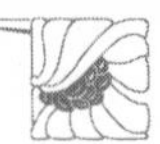

its magickal faerie hour is noon, and its season is summer. Fire is a projective energy, so you can use it to push you forwards and get you noticed – for all the right reasons! It's no accident that those born under a Fire sign like to be the centre of attention and are usually very good at being there too! This is their natural Fire energy projecting out into the world around them.

In magick, Fire spells are cast for protection, transformation, strong cleansings, love, passion, lust, seduction and courage. Because of its unpredictable nature, however, the effects of Fire magick may take you by surprise. Your spells may not work in exactly the way you envisioned, so it is especially important to cast all Fire spells with harm to none (by saying 'I cast this spell with harm to none' at the end of each ritual you perform). Your spells may still have a surprising outcome, but they will carry no negative consequences if you follow this simple guideline.

Attuning with Fire energies is simple. Sunbathe, light a few candles, gaze into the flames of a log fire, enjoy a summer barbecue or a great fireworks party on bonfire night. In the home, the bedroom is the area associated with the spirits of Fire, as it is the place of love, sex and passion. Remember, the key words for Fire energy are protection, power, transformation, love and passion.

Creating a Fire altar

If possible, place your Fire altar in a southern area of your home. Alternatively, set it up in a quiet corner of the bedroom to make the most of the Fire spirits' energies of love and passion. If you choose to use an altar cloth, pick one of red, gold or deep orange. Place two red, gold or orange candles towards the back of the altar as illuminator candles. These should be set in appropriate, sturdy holders.

Now decorate the altar to represent the elementals it is dedicated to. Figures of salamanders, dragons and Fire nymphs are all appropriate. These days you can buy beautiful dragon candleholders designed to hold tea-lights or taper candles. These are perfect for an altar dedicated to the Fire elementals. Add a collection of fiery-coloured crystals such as carnelian, amber and garnet. Some shops sell beautiful lamps of a dragon design; one of these would be an acknowledgement of the salamanders' presence within electricity. Of course, candles of all shapes and sizes are appropriate. If you are a Fire babe, add an ornament to represent your birth sign – a ram for Aries, a lion for Leo or a centaur for Sagittarius. Any sun-shaped ornament will serve to represent the heat of the sun, and any red love heart will represent the Fire spirits' gift of passion. Finally, hang a sun-face wall plaque or a picture of a volcano above your altar as a visual representation of the spirits of Fire and their natural energies.

To invoke the spirits of Fire

Before you can begin working with the elementals of Fire, you will need to invoke them and make their energies welcome in your life and your home.

You will need: Nothing.

Moon phase: Any.

- Go to your altar, cast the circle as described on pages 37–8 and light the two illuminator candles at the back of the altar.
- Stand up tall and raise your arms high above your head, palms facing forwards, in the position of invocation. Now invoke the spirits of Fire into your life by saying the following incantation:

I call on the mighty spirits of non-destructive Fire,
Elementals of passion, protection, power and transformation.
I call your powers through time and space
And invoke your magick within this place.
So mote it be!

You are now ready to work with the Fire elementals.

Dragons

Dragons are the largest elementals of Fire. They can be called on for the strongest forms of protection and to undo magick. They can also be used as personal power animals and totem allies. They are closely connected with the salamander elementals, though the dragons are considered to be the most powerful. They are the keepers of ancient wisdom and can be called upon for strength and courage.

To create a dragon thought form

A dragon thought form can be called upon whenever you feel the need for extra protection. Unlike the Watcher (see pages 31–3), which is used as a daily prevention against danger, the dragon thought form is created when you feel threatened in some way and sense that danger is all around you. This elemental will keep you safe from harm by enfolding you in magickal protection energy. Think of him as a magickal bodyguard!

You will need: Nothing.

Moon phase: Any – whenever you have need of protection.

- Go to your Fire altar, light the illuminator candles and cast the circle as described on pages 37–8.
- Follow the instructions for creating the Watcher thought form on pages 31–3, adapting your visualisation to see instead a magnificent fire-breathing dragon. How you envision him is up to you. He can be any colour. Just make sure he looks like a force to be reckoned with! I personally see my protection dragon as being bright red, with a spined back, barbed tail and flashing amber eyes. Use your imagination and see him clearly and in as much detail as possible.
- Once you have breathed life into your thought form, say the following incantation to activate his powers:

Dragon of power, I summon you here
To take away all my fear.
Keep me safe and keep me calm;
When danger is near, keep me from harm.
Guard me now from every foe
Or your retribution they shall know!
This is my will. So mote it be!

- Now instruct your elemental dragon in his duties. Tell him what danger you face and the nature of your fear.
- See your dragon slowly fade away and disappear to carry out his role. Know that around you you now have the strongest form of magickal protection.
- Reaffirm the protection daily by saying:

Guardian dragon, heed what I say:
Protect and guard me throughout this day!
I cast this spell with harm to none.

To reverse a spell

Occasionally, you may fall into the trap of casting a spell that you later wish you hadn't. Most witches make this mistake at some stage in their magickal life. We've all been there, so don't panic! The trick is ... more magick, in the form of a reversal spell.

When it comes to reversing magick, you can't beat the power of a chaos dragon. He will put a stop to any magickal mess you may have landed yourself in. Being an elemental of chaos, he will create some fallout, but this should be minimal, as you have taken responsibility for your mistake and are doing something about it.

You will need: A black pen, a piece of paper, a black candle, matches or a lighter, your brewing pot or another heatproof dish.
Moon phase: Any – whenever you need to reverse a spell.

- Take all the items to your altar and cast the circle as described on pages 37–8. Light the illuminator candles and breathe deeply for a few moments.
- Using the black pen, write the spell that you originally cast on the piece of paper, then roll the paper into a scroll.

- Light the black candle and call on the powers of the chaos dragon by using the following incantation:

Great chaos dragon,
Bring your power to me.
Reverse this magick.
Let it be!

- Light the spell paper in the candle flame and allow it to burn in the brewing pot or heatproof dish.
- Snuff out the candle and allow the dragon to do his work.

A fire watcher salamander spell

Believe it or not, the best way to use magick to protect your home from accidental fire is to invoke the spirits of Fire. As the salamanders are the rulers of this element, their magickal presence can guard your home from all forms of destructive fire, including electrical faults and lightning bolts. Of course, magick is no replacement for common sense, so you must do all you can in a practical way to safeguard your home. Make sure any faulty wiring is replaced, don't overload plug sockets and observe basic safety rules when using candles and so on. Then use this spell as a magickal back-up.

You will need: A dragon-style tea-light holder, a tea-light.
Moon phase: Full.

- Place the dragon tea-light holder on your altar pentacle to charge for 24 hours.
- On the night of the full moon, light the illuminator candles and cast the circle as described on pages 37–8.
- Take the dragon candleholder in both hands, hold it high above your head and say:

I offer this tool as a channel for the elemental powers of the salamanders. May they protect my home, myself and my loved ones from all forms of destructive fire. Each time this tool holds a burning flame, it is in honour of the spirits of Fire and in thanks to the salamanders for their unceasing protection. This is my will. So shall it be!

- Take down the circle as described on page 38.
- Light a tea-light from the flame of one on the illuminator candles and place this in the dragon holder. Blow out the illuminator candles. Find a safe place on your altar, or maybe on your hearth, where the tea-light can burn down in the holder.
- Burn tea-lights in this place regularly to maintain the power of the spell.

The urge to purge!

There are times in our lives when we feel overwhelmed by all the little things – all those negative aspects of life that no longer serve us and may even be holding us back. These things range from bad habits and negative influences to relationships we've outgrown and careers that no longer challenge us. This is all perfectly normal and is an indication that you have grown as a person and are moving steadily along your personal life path. It is important to keep your life moving forwards, and to enable this to happen you must release what no longer serves you. Try to do so with love and without bitterness; that way you will be putting a positive end to a negative situation.

Spirits of Fire are the perfect allies when it comes to purging yourself of all negative influences. Their greedy flames will consume the essence of the problem, leaving you emotionally detached from it and so in a better position to deal with the situation in the mundane world. If for example, you are feeling restless and bored with your job, you could consign it to the flames, in magickal terms, to open up the path for a career change. In the mundane world you continue to go to work as usual, as the bills still need to be paid, but you will also know that you have set the ball rolling and that your current employment is now a temporary measure until your fabulous new career opportunity comes along! This technique can be applied to any negative aspect or area of your life.

All you need do is write down the negative influence or situation on a slip of paper with a red pen. Roll the paper into a scroll. Light a red candle, then light the spell paper from the candle and allow it to burn in a heatproof dish. As the spell paper burns say:

I call on the spirits of Fire to help me purge this negative influence from my life and make room for something much better! So mote it be!

Once the spell paper has completely burnt, your spell is done and you can set about moving your life forward.

A spell for transformation

A simple act of meditation can help to transform your life.

You will need: A pen and paper.

Moon phase: Any.

- Go to your Fire altar and light the illuminator candles, then cast the circle as described on pages 37–8.
- Breathe deeply for a few moments, until you are centred and relaxed. Then take the pen and paper and write down, in as much detail as possible, a description of your ideal life – or your ideal version of whatever you wish to transform.
- Read the description out loud.
- Close your eyes and visualise yourself living this transformed life. See yourself happy and well and enjoying every moment of this alternative existence.
- Continue for as long as you wish, then when you are ready say:

  By the transformative power of Fire, this is the life I wish to live. I cast this spell with harm to none. This is my will. So mote it be!

- Fold the paper and place it beneath one of the dragon or salamander figures on your Fire altar. Alternatively, place it beneath the candleholder of one of your altar candles.
- For the best results, repeat the spell words and visualisation every night before you go to bed and remember that any kind of transformation takes time. How much time will depend on how elaborate your desired life is and how much personal effort you put into accomplishing it. But know that you have now set the magickal ball rolling!

A Fire nymph spell for passion power

The energies of Fire elementals can be used to increase the passion in your life and to spice up a flagging relationship, filling it with a new fire and rekindling a burning desire. To enhance this spell, wear sexy red lingerie or a beautiful red satin nightdress and perform it in conjunction with the following spell and the Seduction Dance on pages 64–5.

You will need: A figure or picture to represent a Fire nymph (optional), a few red candles (optional).
Moon phase: Any.

- If you are using the Fire nymph representation, place it as close to your bed as you can. Place the candles around the room and light them, to create a romantic and sexy ambience.
- Sit before the Fire nymph representation or before your Fire altar. Envision your Fire nymph (as you see her in your imagination if you are not using a representation) and then repeat the following incantation three times:

Beautiful nymph of radiant Fire,
Fill me with a burning desire.
Grant me your gift of wanton glee;
Set my kundalini free!
From this night and from this hour
I embrace my nymph-like passion power!

- Now see yourself taking on the attributes of the passionate Fire nymph. You are filled with desire for your partner and you are confident in your powers to attract and arouse him!

To turn up the heat in a relationship

Long-term relationships can become stale and boring unless you work to keep the passion alive. If your love life is getting a little predictable, inject a some Fire magick into it and turn up the heat! First perform the spell above and take on the sultry energies of a Fire nymph, then try this one.

You will need: Nothing.

Moon phase: Any.

- Concentrating on the fiery elemental powers you are working with, chant the following incantation, continuing for as long as you can remain focused:

Fiery nymph of passions strong,
Let our love last all night long,
Twisting, trembling, writhing free,
Crying out in ecstasy!
Turn up the heat and make it last.
In love and trust this spell I cast.

- As soon as you are all fired up, go get him, girl!

Give something back ...

When working with the Fire spirits to improve your life, it is important to give something back. This is not so easy as it is with the other elementals, but it can be done. Taking the time to meditate on the flame of a red candle and visualising a world where people are more aware of fire safety is a positive start. Teaching youngsters basic fire precautions or working with your local fire brigade can also act as an indication to these elementals that you are offering them your magickal assistance.

The Mermaid

Creature of grace and beauty so fair,
Of feminine charms so enchanting and rare,
Her lips are of coral, her skin is of pearl,
Her untameable tresses forever unfurl.
See her bright eyes of aquamarine
And her elegant tail of iridescent sheen.
The smell of the surf resides in her hair;
She sings on the shore and her voice lingers there.
A necklace of seashells encircles her throat;
Her hair all around her fans out as she floats.
The spell of her song and the point of her ear
Mark her out as the fey, and when she is near
The wind isn't angry, the moon does not hide,
For she sings with the storm and speaks with the tide.
There in the moonlight she sits on the rocks,
Singing her song and combing her locks,
Aware of her beauty, her charm, her allure,
Sexy and sultry, yet unceasingly pure.
Singing and swimming, she's eternally free,
Beautiful mermaid, femme fatale of the sea!

Spirits of Water

The spirits of Water are collectively called the undines. In Greek legend, Undine was a water faerie. Her name means 'wave'. Undines are probably the best-known elementals, particularly in the form of mermaids and sirens. Their energy is present within every source of water from ocean waves, rivers and streams to springs, wells and even rainfall. Every time you take a shower or relax in a hot bath, you have the opportunity to commune with the undines and to utilise their powers. Each time you drink a glass of water, you are taking their energies into yourself.

Water is vital to our survival and is second only to air in terms of our dependence upon it. As two-thirds of our planet is covered with water, and 70 per cent of our bodies consist of it, it should come as no surprise that even the most sceptical and non-magickal individuals are familiar with these elementals, for who is not acquainted with the legend of the mermaid? The undines speak subconsciously to all of us on a daily basis. Each time we wash, bathe, drink or get caught in a shower, we are interacting with the spirits of Water.

Mermaids and sirens have a dark side too. In some legends they lure sailors down to the bottom of the sea and drown them. However, other legends tell of mermaids saving people from drowning and taking them to shore. This illustrates the changeable nature of this element. Spirits of Water can also manifest themselves as the deadly tidal wave, storm surges, torrential rain and all kinds of floods, from flash flooding to broken damns.

There are lots of different legends regarding the spirits of Water, and these elementals go by many names. Here are just a few of the more interesting ones. In Yorkshire, where I live, there is the legend of a malignant water spirit called the grindylow. Her name is often used to frighten little children into keeping away from dangerous bodies of water! In Scotland there is a salmon-tailed mermaid called Ceasg, who has the power to grant wishes, while Loch Maree is said to be inhabited by Maurie, a benevolent male water spirit. Offerings to him are cast into the water or left by the lochside. In Norway, mermaids are known as havfine, and in Denmark there are tales of mermen called havmand. In Roman mythology there is the tale of an oracular water spirit called Egeria. Mary Player is a malignant English mermaid who sinks ships by swimming around them three times. It is thought to be bad luck to say her name when out sailing for fear it should invoke her presence!

Mermaids and sirens

Mermaids and sirens are strongly associated with feminine charms and beauty. Traditionally, they have long flowing tresses and are irresistible to men. They are the witches of the deep. Their song is said to lure unwary sailors to their death, although, as we've seen, these elementals also have a more benevolent side.

Mermaids and sirens differ slightly from one another in appearance. The mermaid is of female form from her head to her waist, and her lower half is that of a fish, with beautiful iridescent scales and a tail that fans out gracefully where her feet would otherwise be. The siren has the body of a woman from top to bottom. She also has the ability to shapeshift into a large bird. Magickally speaking, the siren links the two realms of water and air, while the mermaid is the guardian of the oceans and all large bodies of water.

Are you a Water babe?

If you were born under one of the water signs, Scorpio, Cancer and Pisces, then you will already have a natural affinity with the spirits of Water and you have the potential to be one super-sexy siren! Being born into this element means that you can be a little temperamental, maybe even moody at times. You are comfortable with your own company and can be something of a dreamer, often getting lost in your own thoughts. You have the ability to see straight to the depths of a situation and to acknowledge what is going on beneath the surface. A shallow show of affection or a superficial front won't fool you at all! Water signs can be very far-seeing. In this they are helped by finely tuned instincts and strong emotional reactions to things.

The undines will speak to you on a subconscious level, urging you to invest in the luxury of a bath spa, walk in the rain, scry in the mists or go for a swim. They encourage you to discover your natural beauty and allure, to grow your hair long and to sing like a siren! These elementals may even be present in your choice of career or home. Perhaps you live by the sea, or near a loch or lake. Maybe you make your living teaching swimming, designing water features and garden ponds or perhaps even selling bathrooms! In some way the spirits of Water will have a strong presence in your life.

If you were born into this element, it is unlikely that you can be away from water for very long without yearning for it. By that I mean that water will be a strong part of your daily life and your home. Maybe you keep tropical fish or have a beautiful pond in your garden. Perhaps you have a water feature in your home or pictures and figures of mermaids. Maybe you drift off to sleep to the strains of an ocean sounds CD.

For us water signs, bathtime is about so much more than simple cleanliness! It is an opportunity to escape, to lie back in the warm comfort of our natural element. Here we can forget the stresses and worries of daily life and dream of a brighter future for ourselves. If, like me, you have always had a fascination with the legends of mermaids and sirens, this is your natural affinity with the Water spirits coming through, and your bathroom is the perfect place to attune with these elementals.

I recently felt inspired to decorate my bathroom, transforming it into something of a sea siren's cove. I used shades of deep blue and ocean jade, hung pictures of mermaids on the walls and placed figures of sexy sirens around the room. My bathroom now has a wonderful magickal feel. It is dedicated to female beauty and innocent allure. The energy here is now so strong that every time I lie relaxing in my bath, I can't help but feel like a bit of a siren myself – at least for a short while! So do pay attention to what your elementals are urging you to do, follow their inspiration and you will soon feel alive with vibrant siren energy!

The magick of Water

In magickal terms, the powers of Water are gentle, and they help us to achieve balance, harmony, inner peace and tranquillity.

This element can also be used to assist in matters of stress relief, dreams, health, psychic powers and gentle cleansings. Attuning with the elementals of Water can help you to discover your inner beauty and powers of attraction. Undines are often the spirit guides of girls and women, for whom they are powerful protectors. Their energies are great for assisting with magickal enchantments, love spells, allure, seduction, sexual confidence, flirting and so on.

The colour associated with water is, obviously, blue. The direction is west, the magickal faerie hour dusk and the season autumn. Water is considered to be a receptive energy, and its tides can pull positive things towards you and negative things away from you. To attune with these elementals, go to the beach, paddle in a stream, walk in the rain, soak in the bath or place a water feature in your home. To ensure that you are working magick that is conducive to the energies of this element, remember its key words: seduction, beauty, enchantment, healing, cleansing, intuition, dreams and psychic ability.

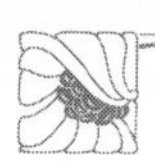

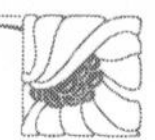

Creating a Water altar

An altar dedicated to the spirits of Water should be placed in the west – or alternatively you might want to set up a small siren shrine (a shrine does not include basic magickal tools) in your bathroom. If you wish to use an altar cloth, choose one of an aquatic colour such as deep blue, jade, turquoise or aquamarine. Place two blue candles towards the back of the altar as illuminator candles. Now decorate the altar so that it represents the elemental energies it is dedicated to.

Figures of mermaids and siren-like ladies are a great start. To these you can add collections of seashells, dried seaweed and starfish, and crystals in various blues and greens. Fill your chalice with spring water. Add a small wishing well ornament to represent the water sprites and well nymphs. Mirrors are often used in magick to represent the element of water, so a small, round make-up mirror would be appropriate.

If you are a Water babe, add an ornament to represent your birth sign – a scorpion for Scorpio, a crab for Cancer or a fish for Pisces. Finally, hang a picture of a mermaid or the crashing ocean waves on the wall above your altar as a visual representation of the spirits of Water and their natural energies.

To invoke the spirits of Water

Before you begin working with the elementals of Water you will need to invoke them and make their energies welcome in your life and your home.

You will need: Nothing.

Moon phase: Any.

- Go to your altar and cast the circle as described on pages 37–8, then light the illuminator candles.
- Raise your arms high above your head, palms facing forwards, in the position of invocation. Now invoke the spirits of Water into your life by saying the following incantation:

I call on the mighty spirits of Water,
Elementals of beauty and seduction, healing and intuition.
I call your powers through time and space
And invoke your magick within this place.
So mote it be!

You are now ready to work any of the spells in this chapter.

Marie Morgana

While doing research for this book I came across a Water elemental that bears both my given name and my magickal name. This came as quite a surprise to me, as these elementals come from a small corner of mythology that I hadn't been aware of before. The Marie Morgana are sea sirens of Breton, Cornish and Celtic folklore. I feel that this might explain the strong affinity I've felt with mermaids and sirens since childhood – though it does make the fact that I'm a non-swimmer a little ironic!

In folklore, the Marie Morgana are artful seductresses who tempt men into their undersea world with the spell of their song. They sleep by day and rise to the surface at night, sitting on moonlit rocks to comb out their hair. They are recognised by the whiteness of their skin, their youthful beauty, their seductive allure and their enchanting singing voice. They are thought to be related to Morgan le Fey and also the Lady of the Lake of Arthurian legend (for more information see Chapter 11). Because of this link, the Marie Morgana are often called the sea-witches, and they are associated with magick and witchcraft, seduction and enchantment. Their mythological cousin is the Fata Morgana, an Italian mermaid who has similar attributes and is thought by some to be a weaver of magick and spinner of destiny.

Creating a Marie Morgana thought form

This thought form can help you to attune with the energies of the Water elementals in general. Alternatively, she can shower you with the gifts she is associated with: seduction, beauty, allure, a fine singing voice and a deep knowledge of the magickal arts. I see this thought form as a beautiful sea siren with long, untamed tresses and dark soulful eyes. Her skin is white, with an iridescent sheen, and she holds a closed oyster shell in her hands. If you feel comfortable with this image, then go ahead and use it, but if you prefer to create your own image of the Marie Morgana, this is fine too. (For the purposes of this spell, your Marie Morgana should be holding an oyster shell.)

You will need: Nothing.
Moon phase: Any.

- Go to your Water altar, light the illuminator candles and cast the circle as described on pages 37–8.
- Follow the instructions on pages 31–3 for creating a thought form, adapting your visualisation to the Marie Morgana holding a closed oyster shell.
- Once you have breathed life into your Marie Morgana thought form, say the following incantation to activate her powers:

Creature of seduction and beauty famed,
Marie Morgana is your name.
Siren of magick, of witchcraft and spell,
Sing me a song and bestow a gift from your shell.

- Ask the Marie Morgana for the gift you desire, choosing

something that she is associated with. For example, you might ask for the gift of innocent allure or the ability to see and nurture your own inner beauty. You could ask for help with music and singing lessons or even the means to buy a Karaoke system so you can sing your siren songs to your heart's content!

- Imagine the oyster shell the Marie Morgana is holding opening up to reveal a pearl. In your mind's eye see yourself taking the pearl as a symbol of the gift you have requested.
- Now see the Marie Morgana fading away in a shimmer of aquamarine light. Your gift should become apparent in your life within three moons. Know that you can call on this Marie Morgana faerie at any time by repeating the incantation above and making your request.

A siren song seduction spell

By far the most powerful spell a mermaid or siren can help you with is a seduction spell. As witches of the deep and mistresses of enchantment and allure, these faerie elementals can do wonders for your self-image. Surrounding yourself with siren energy can help to raise your self-esteem and make you feel beautiful and sexy on any day of the week!

You will need: An image of a mermaid or siren, a CD of ocean sounds (optional), matches or a lighter, incense of a marine fragrance, a photograph of your lover (if you are in a relationship).
Moon phase: Any.

- Take all the items to your altar and cast the circle as described on pages 37–8.
- Light the illuminator candles and incense and put the CD on to play. Place the mermaid figure in the centre of the altar and put the photograph just in front.
- Concentrate on the elemental energy you are working with, using the mermaid as a focus. Invoke the siren as follows:

  Beautiful siren, enchantress and seductress, I ask that you bestow your gifts upon me that I may attract love and passion into my life. Be with me and assist me in my magickal working.

- Now concentrate on the photo of your lover – or if you are not in a relationship, on the qualities of your ideal partner and on bringing him to you. Feel the siren energy around you and imagine that you are absorbing it into yourself – you are becoming a siren!
- When you feel ready, chant the following siren song, continuing for as long as you can remain focused:

Come to me, I summon thee,
Hear now my siren song.
Come to me, I summon thee,
For I have loved thee long.
Swim with me, spin with me,
Live with me and be my love;
Play with me, lie with me,
I'll take you to the stars above.
Dance with me, entranced you'll be;
I cast my witch's web out wide.
Think of me, dream of me;
From my charms you cannot hide!
Look for me, feel for me;
The magick of my spell unfurls.
Teach me, reach out for me;
My love for you will rock your world.
Let me lead you by the hand
To my secret place.
Your will succumbs to my demand,
Crossing time and space.
See my lips, my swaying hips,
Your gaze is locked with mine.
Feel my power, 'tis the hour.
Come now – you are mine!

- Blow out the candles and allow the spell to play itself out in your life. Repeat as desired!

Selkies

In Scottish folklore there are many tales of the seal people known as selkies (pronounced silkies). These magickal creatures are thought to be members of the fey and are related to the sirens, being sea creatures of a shapeshifting nature. Selkies are seals who can take on human shape and walk on land. They usually appear by moonlight in the guise of a beautiful maiden, although more rarely they may appear as handsome young men. They are very magickal and are known to have the gift of healing.

To see a selkie is to fall head over heels in love! However, the only way to bind a selkie to the land is to steal and hide away her seal skin, without which she cannot return to the waves.

The selkie will always be drawn to the sea nevertheless, and should she ever discover her pelt she will immediately return to the ocean. A certain degree of discontent will always be felt by a selkie who is trapped on land. In most tales the selkie will eventually return to her natural home, often leaving behind husband and children. Thus in the following spell, the selkie elemental can help us through the pain of a separation or romantic break-up.

A selkie spell

This spell first appeared in my book *Magical Beasts*. If a love has ended, repeat it daily at dusk until the healing process is complete. This may require some considerable time. An ended love affair can take months or even years to get over, but making or accepting the break is always the hardest part. This little spell will help you to heal yourself and move on with your life. If you live near the sea, spend as much time as you can on the beach and say the spell to the waves.

You will need: Nothing.

Moon phase: Any – work at dusk.

◆ As dusk falls, go to your altar and focus on the image of a seal or selkie. When you see it clearly in your mind's eye, call on the magickal powers of the selkie in the following way:

Selkie, my love and I must part.
Please help me heal this broken heart.
Give me strength to find my way,
For with my love I cannot stay.
Let new joy bubble like the ocean's foam
And let me find my true home.
Selkie, selkie, heal my heart,
For my love and I are world's apart.

Hair

Undines are famed for their preternaturally long hair, and in the popular image they are usually depicted combing out beautiful long locks. Very long hair is said to be a mark of the fey, with red hair being especially potent and magickal. Hair is often used in spells to link the magick with a particular person, and in the past, locks of hair were given to remember the dead or between lovers to strengthen the bond. Faerie folk are said to be recognisable by their hair, which never dries completely and is always left free-flowing.

In witchcraft, hair is a symbol of power and is usually left loose during ritual, unless this would be dangerous, for example in a fire spell. It is said that a woman in labour should leave her hair unbound to 'free' the baby and ensure an easy birth, meaning a birth without any complications. I doubt that there is any such thing as a truly easy birth – they don't call it labour for nothing!

Hair can also be used as a tool of transition. Cutting the hair can mark a rite of passage or indicate a new phase of life. This may be the reason many women feel the need for a restyle after the ending of a relationship. This form of voluntary hair loss can be an empowering statement about your personal self-image. However, hair loss can also come about in less welcome ways, for example as a result of excessive perming or bleaching, because of the condition alopecia or as a consequence of life-saving but invasive chemotherapy treatment. Such hair loss can be traumatic, and it may be difficult to remain positive in the face of it. Try to see such an event as an opportunity to give yourself a makeover and a new image, using clever haircuts, hair pieces and wigs. Even if you are happy with your own hair, wigs are a great way to experiment with new colours and styles, or to be someone else for a day. If it's good enough for the celebrities, it's good enough for you too!

A spell for luscious locks

You will need: A hairbrush of natural bristles (a plastic one will tear and break your hair).

Moon phase: Any.

- Place the hairbrush on your Water altar and say:

  I call on the undines, spirits of Water. I ask that they bless me with the gift of long, luscious locks. So mote it be!

- Leave the hairbrush in place for 24 hours. It can now be used as a tool to brush magick into your hair. Whenever you use the hairbrush, visualise yourself with long, strong, shining locks and say the following brushing chant to strengthen the spell:

  Stronger and longer,
  Longer and stronger,
  Thick and shiny for all to see;

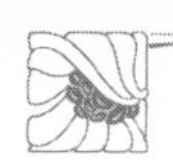

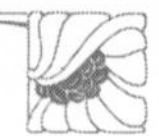

Stronger and longer,
Longer and stronger,
Give me luscious locks. So mote it be!

A spell for beauty

Water is a key ingredient in cultivating your natural beauty. Drinking lots of water will help to keep your skin fresh and clear. Ideally, we should all be drinking about eight glasses of water every day. This spell is a traditional beauty remedy.

You will need: A clean sponge.

Moon phase: Any – work at dawn, in the summer, especially on Midsummer's Day (on or around 21 June), when faerie magick is strongest.

- Rise early and go out into the garden, taking the sponge with you.
- Use the sponge to collect dew by gently wiping it across flowers and leaves in your garden.
- Go back indoors and use the dew to wash your face, as you do so saying:

Spirits of Water, of charm and grace,
Bless me with beauty as I wash my face.

Work this spell daily if you wish.

For enchantment and allure

To increase your sense of personal enchantment and allure, surround yourself with siren energy by filling your home with representations of undines. There are lots of fine art prints available depicting mermaids, sirens and water nymphs. Turn your bathroom into a river siren's retreat and attune with your inner siren there. Or collect figures of mermaids and siren-type women and place them around your home and office. Once siren energy is reflected back at you from every corner of your home, you will begin to absorb this energy on a daily basis.

A sea spell for allure

To further increase your allure, try this spell.

You will need: A necklace or bracelet made of seashells or coral.
Moon phase: Waxing.

- Place the necklace or bracelet on your pentacle to charge, as you do so holding your hands over it, palms down, and empowering it by saying:

Power of the sea, magick of the undines,
Let the gifts of enchantment and allure be mine.
This necklace is a symbol of mermaid style,
Bestowing allure and a radiant smile!

- Leave the necklace in place for 24 hours and then wear it whenever you feel the need to boost your self-image and sense of attractiveness.

A healing spell

To perform this spell you will need to be next to a body of tidal water, preferably the sea, but a river or tidal loch will do. Before you work the spell, ask the person you wish to heal for their permission.

You will need: A seashell, a blue marker pen.
Moon phase: Any.

- Using the marker pen, write the name of the person you wish to heal on the seashell.
- Hold the seashell between your palms and visualise the person you are healing as healthy and fully recovered.
- As the tide ebbs, stare out to sea for a while, imagining the undines.
- Kiss the seashell to empower it with love and then throw it out into sea as far as you can, as you do so saying the following incantation:

I call on the mermaids, the spirits of the sea,
I call their powers here to me.
Take this seashell into the deep

And heal the one whose name it keeps.
In love and trust this spell I sow,
By the power of the tide's ebb and flow.
By the power of the sea, so mote it be!

- Leave the beach without looking back and allow the spell to play itself out in your life and the life of your loved one.

A spell for prophetic dreams and psychic development

Mirrors are often used in magick to symbolise and connect with the powers of Water, and they are thought to create doors to other worlds, particularly the astral realm.

You will need: 3 small, round make-up mirrors; a pen or marker suitable for writing on the back of the mirrors.
Moon phase: Any.

- Take the three mirrors to your altar, cast the circle as described on pages 37–8 and light the illuminator candles.
- Say:

I call on the undines, the spirits of Water, to assist me in this spellcasting.

- Place the three mirrors in a row on your altar. Hold your hands, palms down, over the first and say:

Mirror of magick, portal of power,
Visions of the past come through your door.

- Hold your hands over the second mirror and say:

Mirror of magick, portal of power,
Visions of the present come through your door.

- Hold your hands over the third mirror and say:

Mirror of magick, portal of power,
Visions of the future come through your door.

- On the back of each mirror write past, present or future accordingly. The mirrors can now be used to reflect psychic dreams, images and visions back to you.

- Place the mirrors beneath your bed, as the best time to receive such psychic images is while you are sleeping. If you want to incubate a dream of the past, present or future, place the corresponding mirror beneath your pillow and leave it there for a few nights until your psychic vision has manifested in your dreams. Then place the mirror back under the bed with the others and give thanks to the undines.

A spell for protection against unwanted admirers

While the attentions of an admirer can at first be quite flattering, they can quickly become a pain in the neck! When you work with the undines and surround yourself with siren energy, you will invariably attract male attention! However, the sirens understand that not all masculine attention is welcome and they will happily come to your rescue if you work this spell.

You will need: A seashell for each unwanted admirer, a pen.
Moon phase: Waning.

- Take the seashell(s) to a beach, stream or river.
- Write the name of one admirer on each shell and then cast the shells one by one into the body of water, as you cast each shell saying:

Undines take away this man;
Free me from his gaze.
Turn his head and help him see
Through his lovesick haze
That he and I are not meant to be
And let another fill his days.
I cast this spell with harm to none.
So mote it be!

- Return home and wait for the spell to play out in your life.

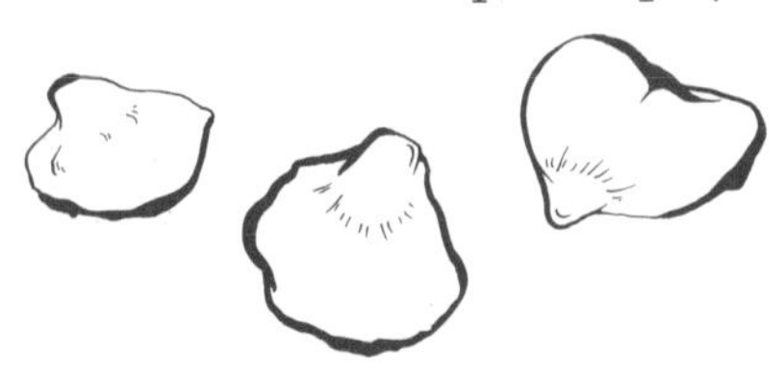

Give something back …

When working with the spirits of Water to improve your life, it is important to give something back. This means being more aware of water pollution issues and being very careful what you put down your drains! Some detergents are extremely harmful to the environment, so do check before you pull the plug! A more magickal way to give something back to the spirits of Water is to work the following spell as often as you can.

A spell to cleanse the oceans

As you are probably aware, the waters of the world are very badly polluted, and as humans made the mess, it's up to us to clean it up! Call on the undines and ask that they take the energy you give in this spell and use it to cleanse the oceans, rivers and streams of our planet.

You will need: A bowl, a bottle of pure spring water, some blue or green food colouring.
Moon phase: Any.

- Fill the bowl with the spring water and add a drop or two of the food colouring to make it look like a beautiful enchanted pool.
- Sit with the bowl of water on your knee and place both hands in the water. Gently move them around, feeling the softness of the liquid gliding through your fingers.
- Now visualise a strong white light beaming out from your fingertips into the water. This is your magickal energy.
- Next imagine a tiny mermaid swimming up and taking this energy from you. Visualise her swimming off to use your energy where it is most needed in the waters of the world.
- Pour the water into a stream or river, or down the drain, so that it can join up with the oceans later on its journey.

Elf Song

Elven ones of grace so rare,
Of gentle eyes and golden hair,
Skilled in herb, wood and metal,
Seeing wisdom in each unfolding petal,
Who know the teachings of the stars,
May your friendship soon be ours.
And in the woods at dead of night
Elven Lords may come in sight,
And on the wind at break of day,
You may hear a whisper say:
'Treat all nature with respect
Or our teachings you reject.
Learn from beast, bud and leaf,
Give thanks for every golden sheaf.
Hear now the wisdom of the elves:
Put love of nature before yourselves.'

Faces in the Bark

Forests and woodlands are filled with the energies of natural magick. Faeries and elementals have long been associated with densely wooded areas and thick tangled undergrowth. In every woodland, elementals such as dryads, nymphs, elves and satyrs reside. It is in the forest that the Wiccan deities known as Mother Nature (or the Lady of the Woods) and the Green Man (or the Lord of the Trees) can best be attuned with.

Most of you will be familiar with the concept of woodland elves and forest faeries. There are lots of woodlands spirits and they are called by different names in different parts of the world. Here are a few that you may not be so familiar with.

In Russia, the rusalka are wood nymphs who are believed to be the spirits of unwed mothers. They appear as beautiful blond-haired women, dressed in gowns made from green leaves and other foliage. Their appearance is said to be a warning against promiscuity, though they are also linked with fertility.

In England and Scotland, the heather pixies are said to reside in vast tracts of moorland, while the woodwose is a male forest spirit of Anglo-Saxon origin who shares many of the Green Man's attributes. Elves are known by other names too. An Old English name for the woodland elves is wyldaelfen, while in Switzerland they are called the vattaren.

In Scandinavia, the forest faeries are known as wood wives, while in Germany the Wilde Fräulein is a wood nymph associated with the turning seasons. In Denmark, Vette was a beautiful wood nymph who sang enchanting spell songs.

Greek mythology is full of tales of nymphs and dryads, including Dryope, a beautiful nymph who was loved by the amorous sun god Apollo. Another wood nymph, called Daphne, was also pursued by this god. She eventually transformed into a laurel tree in order to escape him.

This wealth of mythology illustrates that the concept of forest spirits is by no means new, but has been a part of world folklore for centuries.

The magick of the forest

As the largest plants on our planet, trees hold an immense power and energy. The turning of the seasons is indicated by the changing foliage of the trees – buds and blossoms in springtime, full leafy branches in summer, crisp golden leaves fluttering to the forest floor in autumn, and the bare branches of winter standing black and stark against the snow-laden sky. The trees around us act as barometers of the seasons and great purifiers of the atmosphere, taking in carbon dioxide and breathing out oxygen. They provide wood for building, fruit and nuts as tasty snacks, welcome shade on a hot summer's day, and cosy retreats for the wildlife.

Trees also hold a key place in magick and witchcraft. They provide wood for wands, brooms and staffs; valuable oils and resins for use in magickal rituals; and ingredients for medicinal purposes too. Symbolically, trees link the different realms, their roots being deeply grounded in the earth or Underworld, their trunks standing firmly in our own realm of Middle Earth, and their branches reaching high up to the heavens and the Otherworld. In some cultures, spiritual traditions are based on a Tree of Life, for example the Jewish Kabbalah and the Norse Yggdrasil.

Trees are connected with all levels of life and with each of the four elements. Their roots anchor them to Earth, they take nourishment from Water, they photosynthesise the Fire of the sun into food, and they provide oxygen for the atmosphere – and lofty homes for the creatures of Air. As the earthly representative of the spiritual Tree of Life, they are also linked with the fifth element of Spirit, or Akasha.

In Celtic tradition, each month is linked to a specific tree – this is known as the Celtic tree calendar. This concept is echoed in Norse tradition too, in which each rune is linked to a specific tree. The Druids are well known for their special affinity with all trees, particularly the oak. They used the Ogham alphabet to strengthen this link and to attune with the trees' elemental energies. To the Native American Indians, trees are their siblings of the earth and are called the Standing People. In their tradition, trees are associated with Earth power and the direction of north, and this is echoed in some Wiccan traditions.

Trees have a profound effect on all of us, for without them it would be impossible for us to breathe the atmosphere. They also have a spiritual effect on us, whether or not we are conscious of it. We are all naturally drawn to trees. Why are children and dog walkers drawn to the woods? Why do so many faerie tales take place in a deep, dark forest? Why, with all the technology the modern world has to offer, do some people still find entertainment and retreat in an old tree house? I believe it is because trees and woodlands exude a powerful natural magick that even the most sceptical person will pick up on some level.

To feel this magick for yourself, take a walk through any woodland or forest and become aware of the peaceful magick of the trees seeping into your veins, exhilarating your senses and inducing a general feeling of well-being. I love to go riding through the woods. If you have a horse, you can attune with the spirits of the forest on your daily ride. Open your mind and your heart and breathe in the magick of the day. The woodland elementals are waiting for you to call upon them, and they will assist you in your spells and rituals. To ensure that you are working magick that is conducive to their energies, remember their key words: strength, growth, resilience and reaching for new heights.

Creating a woodland altar

A woodland altar can be created either indoors or outdoors. An outdoor altar will be very simple and should be placed beneath a tree. An old stump would make an ideal altar surface. Honour the woodland spirits by leaving an earthenware bowl of nuts, seeds and dried fruit here regularly for the wildlife. Collect fallen petals and berries and scatter these on your altar too.

An indoor altar will be more decorative and will hold all your magickal tools. It is also a great way to bring the magickal energies of the wildwood into your home. Here you will be able to attune with the woodland elementals, even if you live far from a forest. A wildwood altar can be very beautiful, and there are lots of lovely items commercially available to decorate such a space.

Your altar surface should be made of wood and left unadorned, so don't use an altar cloth. Gifts of the woodland should be placed in baskets and displayed on or around the altar. Fallen leaves, pine cones, conkers, acorns, berries, fallen blossom and so on are all appropriate. Collect naturally fallen twigs and arrange them in a wooden vase. You might like to hang faceted crystals and faerie charms from the twigs too.

Take a look in any gift store or shopping centre and treat yourself to extra-special candleholders fashioned to look like trees, oak leaf men, or pine cone pixies. These look lovely on a woodland altar. Statues of dryads, satyrs and fairies in leaf dresses could all be used too. Burn a woodland incense such as pine, apple, blackberry or bayberry. Add a pagan altar figure such as Pan, Herne the Hunter, Sabd the deer goddess or Robin Hood. Finally, hang a picture of a beautiful woodland scene or a Green Man plaque on the wall above the altar as a visual connection to the magickal wildwood.

To invoke the spirits of the wildwood

Before you begin working magick with the elementals of the wildwood, you will need to invoke them and welcome their energies into your life and your home.

You will need: Nothing.

Moon phase: Any.

- Go to your woodland altar, cast the circle as described on pages 37–8 and light the illuminator candles.
- Stand in the position of invocation, with your arms upraised and your palms facing forwards, and invoke the spirits of the wildwood by saying the following incantation:

I call on the spirits of the wildwood,
Elementals of growth, strength and resilience.
I call your powers through time and space
And invoke your magick within this place.
So mote it be!

You are now ready to work any of the spells in this chapter.

The Lady of the Woods

Although, in magickal terms, the energies of the woodland are predominantly male, as in all life female energy is also present in order to maintain universal balance and polarity. To witches this female energy is an aspect of the Great Goddess or Mother Nature. In my own Craft tradition I call this aspect of the Goddess the Lady of the Woods. The poem that appears on page 40, 'Green Lady of the Forest', was inspired by the female energy that is subtly present in wooded areas and forests, and this is how I see this particular aspect of the Goddess.

To attune with the Lady of the Woods

You will need: Nothing.

Moon phase: Any – if possible, work at dawn or dusk.

- Go out to a woodland, if possible at one of the faerie hours (dusk and dawn), when the elemental energy is naturally heightened.
- Sit quietly beneath a tree and say the following charm three times, out loud or in your head if you prefer:

Green Lady of the forest,
I send you this plea:
Please give me a sign
That you're here with me.

- Remain seated and be aware of any movement or other sign that your spell has been heard – a leaf fluttering into your lap, a twig snapping though you appear to be alone, the sudden appearance of wildlife and so on. These are all indications that the Green Lady has heard you and is willing to communicate.
- Stay and commune with the Green Lady for as long as you wish, then give silent thanks and return home, taking with you any natural gift that may have fallen into your lap or at your feet.

The Green Man

The Green Man is the pagan spirit of masculine energy in nature. His face is a mask of foliage with eyes peeping out. In some depictions, leaves even grow out of his mouth and nose. He is the untamed heart of the forest and woodland and the primitive energy of nature. He teaches us about the cyclical nature of the universe – of life, death and rebirth, and that all must die in order to be reborn. Like other pagan deities, the Green Man has multiple personalities! He has been sanitised and adapted over the years, and his alter egos include Puck, Robin Goodfellow, Jack in the Green and Robin Hood. The corn deity John Barleycorn is also an aspect of the Green Man, as is the Green Knight in Arthurian legend.

In pagan tradition, the seasonal lords who rule over the light and dark halves of the year are known as the Oak King and the Holly

King. Each solstice they battle each other for supremacy and for the right to champion the Goddess. At the winter solstice the Oak King wins the battle and sets about bringing in the light half of the year. At the summer solstice the Holly King returns to challenge the Oak King once more. This time the Holly King wins, to bring us the dark half of the year, allowing the earth to rest and sleep.

There are many legends surrounding the Green Man in all his aspects, so if this area of folklore interests you, then do read as much as you can about him. In magick he is called upon for protection, resilience and acceptance and to help us better understand the world around us. The following spell can help you to accept changes in your own life, just as the Green Man accepts the seasonal changes in his environment.

A Green Man spell for acceptance

Sometimes things happen that we cannot change. Learning to accept change can be difficult, but in the long term acceptance will invariably open more doors for us than resistance. In accepting a change we deal with it more quickly and then move on. This makes us more aware of and open to new opportunities. If you are struggling to come to terms with something in your life, call on the Green Man for assistance.

You will need: Nothing.
Moon phase: Any.

- Go to your altar, cast the circle as described on pages 37–8 and light the illuminator candles.
- Sit for a moment thinking about what has come to pass in your life that you are finding it difficult to deal with. Then call on the Green Man in the following way:

I call on the Green Man, Lord of the Trees. I ask that you fill me with your power and strength and that you give me the courage to accept — (state what you need to accept). Fill me with your light and grace and help me through this difficult time. This is my will. So mote it be!

- Remain in contemplation at your altar for as long as you need to. Then give thanks, blow out the candles, take down the circle (as described on page 38) and go about your day.

Dryads

Although dryads originated in Greek mythology, they have been accepted into the folklore of many different cultures. There are two types of dryad. One is a wood nymph who can wander the forest freely. The other – the type we are most familiar with – is the hamadryad. The hamadryad is attached to a particular tree, and although she can leave her tree for short periods of time, she will cease to exist if she stays away too long. Should the tree be damaged or cut down, she takes on the injury too and dies with her tree. This illustrates clearly the magickal truth behind the folklore that the elemental dryad is the life force of her tree. When talking about dryads, magickal people usually refer to the first kind as a wood nymph to differentiate between the two. The spells below utilise the powers of the hamadryad and her tree.

Although in Greek mythology Drus (meaning 'tree') is a male dryad and tree spirit, in general dryads and wood nymphs are considered to be the handmaidens and companions of Artemis, the goddess of the moon and witchcraft, and so are viewed as female energies. They are generally depicted as being female to the waist, with the long flowing hair of the fey, usually of a chestnut-brown or auburn colour. Their legs become part of the tree trunk, with their feet disappearing into the roots and their arms stretching out as branches.

The energies of a dryad are calming and gentle, though if a person intends any harm to the tree or the surrounding area, they may make them feel uneasy or unwelcome. Dryads are a wonderful source of elemental power and excellent companions in magick.

Remember to keep your visualisation strong and clear as you work the following spells.

A dryad spell to heal

This is a very simple spell to perform and it will give you an excuse to get out into a local forest or woodland. Ask for the permission of the person you are working for before you perform this spell.

You will need: A pretty gift tag, a short length of blue ribbon.
Moon phase: Any.

- Write the name of the person who is ill on the gift tag and thread the blue ribbon (blue is the colour of healing magic) through the tag.
- Taking the tag, go to the woods and walk until you find a tree with low-hanging branches. You will feel quite drawn to a particular tree.
- Carefully tie the gift tag to a tree branch, then place your power hand (the one you write with) on the trunk of the tree, so touching wood for luck, and say the following charm:

Dryad residing in this tree,
Please heal the one dear to me
By the power of your elemental energy.
This is my will. So mote it be!

- Give silent thanks to the tree and continue your walk through the woods before returning home.

A dryad spell for growth

You will need: Nothing.

Moon phase: Waxing.

- Go to a wood and sit beneath your favourite tree – or sit beneath a tree in your garden if you prefer. Close your eyes and breathe deeply, opening your mind and heart to connect with the tree spirit.
- Once you can clearly visualise the elemental dryad, state what it is you wish to grow. This could be your savings account, your child, your pet or your own personal growth.
- Chant the following chant, continuing for as long as you can remain focused:

By dryad power this spell I sow.
I've named the thing I wish to grow.
As I do will, it shall be so!
I chant the spell and let it go!

A dryad spell for resilience

Trees are incredibly resilient. In the strongest wind or gale they bend and sway, shiver and dance – but rarely does a strong, healthy tree fall due to elemental forces. We can call on this natural dryad strength and use it in our own lives. Whether you are faced with a particular challenge or are struggling through a difficult time, try this simple spell.

You will need: Nothing.

Moon phase: Any.

- Call to your mind the image of a beautiful dryad. Hold this visualisation firmly in your mind and focus on the gifts of resilience and strength as you chant the following charm:

Bend, don't break, bend, don't break;
Life's hardest knocks I can take.
Straighten spine and thicken skin,
Feel dryad strength in every limb.

To bend beneath the wind I'll learn,
For even the harshest wind must turn.

- Repeat this visualisation and charm as often as you need to.

A dryad spell to attain new heights

Dryads can be called on to help you achieve long-term goals and attain new heights in your career or on your life path.

You will need: A luggage label, a pen.

Moon phase: Any.

- Write down your long-term goals on the luggage label – which symbolises the fact that you are certainly going somewhere!
- Take the label out into the woods and find a young tree – one that will have to grow fast and strive to reach the sunlight. Tie the luggage label to the tree and say:

Youthful dryad of this tree,
Here is my goal for all to see.
As you strive to reach the light,
So help me to attain new heights!

- Return home and know that as the tree grows strong and tall, you will be inspired and assisted upon your chosen path.

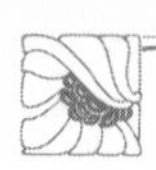

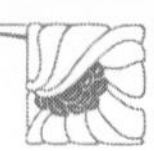

Elves

Elves have recently become one of the more popular elementals. This is largely due to their appearance in Tolkien's books and, more recently, the *Lord of the Rings* epic film trilogy. Now even non-magickal people are aware of elves and their otherworldly beauty. The word 'elf' comes from the Anglo-Saxon aelf and may originally have alluded to a shining angelic being of some kind. In modern times, however, an elf is a woodland elemental, usually tall and willowy, with an androgynous beauty. They can be either male or female in form, but both have the pointed ears that mark them out as members of the fey.

Elves are usually communed with in woodland groves. In British folklore they are said to live in groups, and are always dressed in shades of green, white, silver and gold. They also wear the colours of nature – berry, brown, faun and tan – and dress in natural fabrics such as fur. They have the ability to shapeshift and the gift of premonition and foresight.

Elves are great craftspeople, making items of incredible beauty. Interestingly, they are thought to be one of a very few faeries (the dwarves being another) who can touch and work with metal. Elves are also excellent archers. Their magickal arrows are called elf bolts and they never miss their mark.

Tradition states that should you wake with your hair in a tangle of knots, you have been visiting with the elves in the night. These tangles are known as elf locks. Should elf locks be found in a horse's mane, it is said that the animal has been ridden by the elves in the night and should be allowed to rest the following day.

Release your inner elf

There is no doubt that elves have a beauty and elegance that is all their own. Just as the sirens can help you to become more seductive and sexually confident, so the elves can be called upon to lend their gift of grace. So release your natural beauty by becoming an elven babe in the woods! Dress in the shades of the woodland: greens, browns, tans and berry. Let your wardrobe reflect the dappled beauty of the forest. And try to choose fabrics that the elves might be familiar with, such as suede, wool and a touch of faux fur (please make sure it's not real fur, as the fur trade goes against the Wiccan Rede and the ethics of responsible witchcraft). Add a touch of velvet, a wisp of chiffon, a soft pair of boots and a faux fur bag and you will have captured the essence of elven beauty. Now for the magick!

Just before you go out with your new elf-style look, stand before a mirror and say:

I take on the essence of elven grace;
Natural beauty shows in my face.
Wild, untamed, graceful and free,
A true babe of the wood I wish to be!

Finally, spray on a woody-fragranced perfume and slick on a berry-tinted lip balm and you're good to go!

Pixies

Pixies are the smaller cousins of the elves. They are associated largely with the English West Country, where many local beauty spots are named after them. In terms of magick, they are linked with the Earth elementals and can be called upon to guide a lost traveller. However, they are also quite mischievous and will lead people astray in the woods, making them lose their way and go around in circles. This is known as being pixie-led. A classic sign that you are pixie-led is being able to see the road or path but being unable to get to it no matter how you try! To avoid this situation, say the following little charm whenever you go walking in the woods:

Pixie led I will not be,
For I am a powerful witch you see.
With every step I find my way,
For I am a friend to the fey!

Tradition also states that you should turn your coat inside out and wear it that way if you suspect you are being pixie-led – you will then be able to find your way!

Satyrs

Satyrs are the nature spirits of meadows and woodlands. They are the companions of Pan and they are associated with fun, frolic and sexual liberty. They have the upper body of a man, and the legs, tail and cloven hooves of a goat. From their brow grows a pair of little horns, and their hair and beards are soft and curly. Of course, it's easy to see how this image of the fun-loving satyr became demonised by the early Christians and given the name Satan!

Satyrs link together the realm of man and beast. They have a wild untamed energy and they are the guardians of the woods and the protectors of wildlife. The best-known satyr of all is Pan, the trickster god, who is renowned for his sexual appetite and gift of fertility. The word 'panic' comes from this god – and he will make people panic if they have a negative intent towards the woods and wildlife.

A satyr spell to increase joy

You will need: Nothing.

Moon phase: Waxing.

- Go to your woodland altar, cast the circle as described on pages 37–8 and light the illuminator candles.
- Settle down, close your eyes and call to your mind the image of a satyr. Focus on him as you chant the following charm:

Satyr with your playful ways,
Let joy and laughter fill my days.
Let me frolic and let me play,
And help me chase my cares away!

Give something back ...

As you will by now be aware, it is important to give a little back to the elementals you are working with. Woodland elementals are trying hard to protect our sacred forest and natural beauty spots. Dryads are suffering due to deforestation. So please do your bit. Buy recycled paper and card, and recycle your own household waste. Plant a tree in your garden or go on a tree planting day. Sign petitions against deforestation and for the protection of all our ancient woodlands, such as Sherwood. Visit Sherwood, and other ancient woods, as often as you can to ensure they remain open to the public. Make your voice heard on environmental issues that are important to you and to our planet. The forest elementals will reward you tenfold!

The Tale of Echo

I once was a nymph ... I once was a nymph
Of beauty fair ...beauty fair.
Now all that is left ... all that is left
Is my voice in the air ... in the air, in the air.
I would dance with the breeze ... dance with the breeze
And sing to the flowers ... sing to the flowers.
I would speak with the rain ... speak with the rain
And sleep in the bower ... in the bower, in the bower.
And then he came ... and then he came,
Narcissus, my love ... my love, my love,
And since that day ... since that day
I pined for his love ... his love, his love.
Never once did he see ... never once did he see
The beauty of Echo ... Echo, Echo,
So I froze in the mountains ... I froze in the mountains
And became but an echo ... echo, echo.
The gods in reprisal ... the gods in reprisal
Turned him into a flower ... a flower, a flower,
And there he still blooms ... there he still blooms
On the edge of my bower ... my bower, my bower.
If my true love Narcissus ... Narcissus, Narcissus
You ever should see ... should see, should see,
Take him into your heart ... take him into your heart
In remembrance of me ... of me, of me,
For we played in your childhood ... we played in your childhood
In the mountains and hills ... the mountains and hills,
And you sang with me, Echo ... Echo, Echo,
And I echo there still ... still, still, still ...

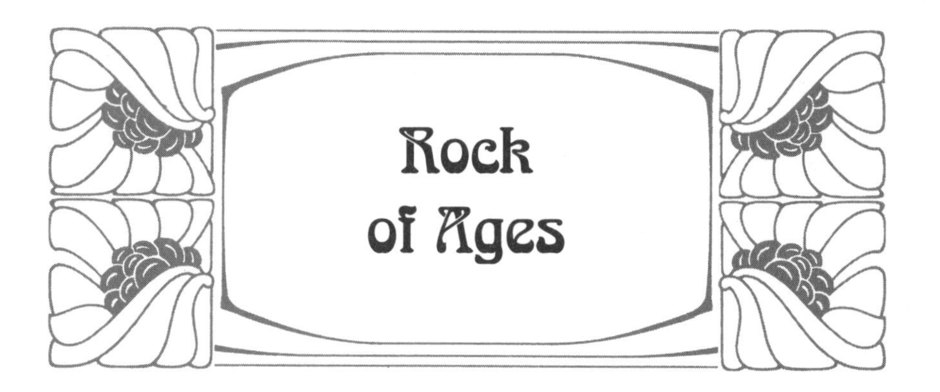

Rock of Ages

You have only to think of the mystery of Stonehenge or the majesty of Ben Nevis to realise that stones, rocks and mountains have a powerful magick of their own. Their longevity is remarkable, and it is highly probable that the mountains and megaliths of Britain will still be standing long after you and I have turned to dust and ashes! Such places have a powerful magickal aura and they have long been associated with faerie sightings and elemental activity.

Elemental guardians of standing stones are called by many names. In Breton folklore the standing stone faeries are called the couril. In France they are the crions, while in the old Gallic tradition they are the vihans. Here in Britain they are called the korreds. In Greek mythology the mountain nymphs are called oriades. The best-known of these is Echo, and hers is a classic tale of unrequited love and the quiet despair and heartbreak that goes with it.

The magick of rock and stone

The concept of the pet rock may seem amusing to twenty-first-century people, but in the past shamans and tribespeople would commune with the energies of rocks and stones in order to forge a spiritual and magickal link with the landscape. Even today, witches and magickal practitioners use stones and crystals in their spells and rituals, and sometimes to define the sacred space of a cast circle. In both instances the practitioner is attuning with the elemental energies of the rock faeries. In terms of magick, such beings can help us to develop a new attitude to the concept of time and to come to terms with our own mortality in a positive way. They can teach us the magick of inner strength and empowerment, and can help us to develop these qualities in ourselves.

However, unless you live close to a stone circle or in a mountainous region, you will need to be inventive when it comes to working with rock faeries. Attuning with them and gaining a sense of who they are requires good visualisation skills. If you meditate, you could try journeying or pathworking to meet one of these elementals on the astral plane. If not, collect natural stones, rocks, pebbles and crystals as you come across them. By placing such items on your altars and around your home you are inviting the rock faeries into your life. Spend holiday time in mountainous regions – I can't look at the Scottish Highland mountains without wishing my arms were long enough to hug them and take in their awesome might and strength! Make a special trip to visit one of the stone circles that are dotted around the UK. Finally, ensure that any magick you cast with these elementals is conducive to their natural energies by remembering their key words: strength, empowerment, standing firm and timelessness.

Standing stones

Ancient standing stones are great for attuning with faeries and elementals. These stones are the power points of natural magick, and some have interesting myths and legends attached to them. The

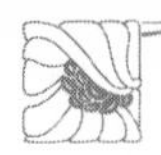

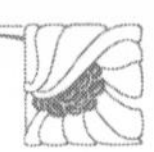

Rollright Stones in Oxfordshire, for example, are said to be a bewitched king and his company of knights. They stand in a circle with a smaller group of stones – known as the Whispering Knights – close by. These are believed to be oracular stones and may whisper your fortune!

The Haltadans are a circle of stones at Fetlar in the Shetlands. Legend states that these stones were once trolls who danced till dawn, when the rays of the rising sun turned them to stone. On the Isle of Skye are two natural stone pillars (although one has now fallen over). Legend states that they were once a husband and wife out looking for lost cattle. They came across a magickal giant who turned them to stone.

Of all the standing stones and megaliths of Britain, Stonehenge is the most famous. Although it is more than 4,000 years old, we are still none the wiser as to its original purpose, or even how it came to be constructed. Was it a temple and place of ritual? Was it some sort of calendar attuned with the seasons and the stars? Was it a place of human sacrifice? The truth is that we will probably never know for certain, and we can only ever make an educated guess. But Stonehenge will always be a place associated with mystery, enchantment, pagan magick and faerie activity, and it is never more popular than on the summer solstice, or Midsummer's Day ...

Midsummer

Immortalised in Shakespeare's play *A Midsummer Night's Dream*, midsummer (on or around 21 June) is the time of year when all faerie power is strongest.

This is a time of magick and enchantment, and it is associated with witches as well as elemental beings. To witches the summer solstice is a time of celebration, when we enjoy the sabbat of Litha. The sabbat festivities usually involve some form of faerie magick, such as the spell below. It is also traditional to make a pilgrimage to the site of ancient standing stones and attune with the energies there. If this isn't possible for you, try the following spell to encourage faerie dreams.

A midsummer night's dream spell

The purpose of this spell is to help you see the rock faeries in your dreams.

You will need: 4 rose quartz crystals, a lantern and tea-light, matches or a lighter, a saucer of milk.
Moon phase: Any – work on Midsummer's Eve.

- At dusk on Midsummer's Eve, go into your garden and cast a circle by marking the four cardinal points with the four crystals.
- Sit in the middle of the circle and light the tea-light, placing it in the lantern before you. Now say:

Faeries, I call you, as dusk follows light,
Walk into my dreams on midsummer's night.
Teach me your secrets and fill me with light,
And lend me your gift of second sight.

- Stay in the circle for as long as you wish to, enjoying the beauty of the summer's evening. Then carefully step out of the circle, leaving the crystals and lantern in place, along with the saucer of milk as an offering for the fey.
- Go inside and go straight to bed. You should see the rock faeries in your dreams within the next three nights.

Queen Mab

Mab is the faerie queen of Celtic folklore. She is particularly associated with the Welsh faeries, though she is known in Scotland and parts of England too. She is a queen of magick and enchantment and is linked with midwifery. Like many of the fey, Mab has been viewed as both good and evil, and she is often depicted as something of a trickster. At her darkest and most negative, she is said to steal babies from their crib and to be the true mother of all changelings. Some believe that she derived from the Irish goddess Maeve or that she has links with the Morrigan. Certainly there are similarities between all three deities, and it could be that these are regional names for the same goddess. Queen Mab is strongly associated with circles of standing stones, and legend states that to call out her name three times in such a place will invoke her presence.

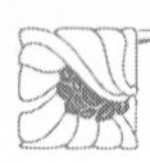

To create a Queen Mab thought form

As an elemental thought form Queen Mab can guide you on your path of faerie magick. She may inspire you to visit a particular place or encourage you to work with a specific type of elemental. Her guidance will come to you in dreams, for she is the keeper of visions. Keeping a dream journal may help you to recognise her signs and communications.

You will need: Nothing.
Moon phase: Any.

- Go to your altar, cast the circle as described on pages 37–8 and light the illuminator candles.
- Follow the instructions for creating the Watcher on pages 31–3, adapting your visualisation to see a beautiful, tall faerie lady. She is regal and stately and is dressed in a gown of deep purple velvet. Her long black hair falls to her knees and is tucked back behind the pointed ears of the fey. On her head she wears a silver and white crown that sparkles like icicles and diamonds. Her lips are berry-red and she has preternatural violet eyes.
- Breathe life into this thought form and then say the following incantation to activate her powers:

Powerful Mab, Faerie Queen,
Guide me with your gift of dreams.
Queen of magick, give me a sign
To help me on this path of mine.

- In your mind's eye see Queen Mab bow her head and then fade away in a shimmer of violet light. Take careful note of your dreams from now on, as there may be a message within them from the Faerie Queen.

Crystals

One of the best ways to attune with the rock faeries is to use crystals in your magickal spells. These are widely available from gift shops and New Age and occult stores, and even some department stores. There are many varieties to choose from. The following is a basic list to get you started.

Clear quartz: For cleansings and clarity
Snowy quartz: For angel spells and purity
Rose quartz: For love, romance and trust
Smoky quartz: For mild banishings and bindings
Tiger's eye: For protection, Earth spells and feline magick
Amethyst: For healing, psychic ability and dream work
Aventurine: For gnome spells, fertility and abundance
Citrine: For sylph spells, communication and concentration
Carnelian: For salamander spells, passion and seduction
Turquoise: For undine spells, intuition and emotional release
Moonstone: For feminine issues and empowerment

Crystals are a great way to bring magick into the office or to communal areas of the home in a pretty and discreet way. Fill a glass bowl with sand to create a soft bed and then lay your crystals on the surface. Choose the crystals carefully and focus on your magickal goal as you arrange them – for example, better communication between you and your colleagues at work. By using crystals in this way you are tapping into the elemental powers of the rock faeries.

Care of crystals

Crystals are quite fragile, so do be careful not to drop them – they chip and break easily. Keep your crystals in a safe place, such as a felt-lined box or drawer – a jewellery box or casket is ideal. Do not allow your crystals to come into direct contact with salt, as this will eventually corrode them and is harmful to their magickal energies.

Cleansing crystals

It is important to keep your crystals physically and psychically clean if you want to get the best magickal results. Most witches cleanse their spell crystals after the manifestation of the spell has occurred. The spell crystal is then put carefully away until the next time its magick is required.

The best way to clean your crystals is to run them under tepid water for a few minutes and then lay them on a soft towel and place them in a sunny spot, such as a windowsill, to dry. If you have to put them outside, keep a close eye on them – I have given lots of crystals to the pair of magpies who live in my garden! Magpies, crows and rooks all love shining, glittering objects, so if you leave your crystals outdoors, be willing to share them!

Empowering crystals

Once you have cleansed your crystals, you will need to empower them so that they are ready once more for magickal work. The best way to do this is to leave them on a windowsill for the three nights of full moon energy. This will charge them with the natural power of the moon. Once you have laid out all your crystals for charging, hold your hands over them, palms down, and say:

In your name, Mother Goddess, I bless these crystals and infuse them with your power. So mote it be!

As soon as the moon begins to wane, put your crystals away safely until you need their power.

Using a pendulum

A great way to use the power of the rock faeries is to work with a pendulum. Choose a crystal pendulum that appeals to you. Good ones to try are clear quartz, rose quartz and amethyst. Once you have chosen your pendulum, learn how to use its power. Sit quietly and hold the chain of the pendulum firmly but gently. Now ask the pendulum to show you a positive answer. Note the way the pendulum moves – this means 'yes'. Now do the same thing again, this time asking for a negative answer. The change in movement indicates 'no'. Now that you know how your pendulum moves for yes and no (and note that this is slightly different for everyone), you are ready to use it in your divinations. Begin by saying the following charm three times:

Gentle faerie of this stone,
Tell me what I wish to know.
As you swing out to and fro,
Give me an answer – yes or no.

Now ask your question and note the way the pendulum moves. Ensure that you ask only yes/no questions or the reading could become very confusing!

Mountain nymphs

The following two spells call on the oriades, the mountain nymphs. Make sure you can visualise these elementals clearly in your mind before you begin. There is no right or wrong way to do this. Go with your first instinct, which is usually correct.

A spell to bend the time

Mountain elementals can help us to understand that time is a relatively man-made concept. Bending time is a magickal phrase that means shaping time slightly to our will so that it works for us, not against us. This spell won't alter time, but it will make it work in your favour. It shouldn't be used too often, as it subtly changes the fabric of life, but it is a safe spell to perform every once in a while.

I created this spell so that I could finish work early when I worked in an office and was part of the nine-to-five rat race. Feel free to adapt it and reword it to better suit your own time-bending needs! It always worked for me, sometimes allowing me to finish work up to two hours early! Here's how it's done ...

You will need: Nothing.
Moon phase: Any.

- In your mind, call on the mountain faeries to help you bend the time for your own specific purpose.
- Visualise a large pentagram of flames filling the door to your office or work area. Visualise another flaming pentagram engulfing the telephone. Now chant the following charm in your head repeatedly – keeping it up until your boss lets you go:

Bar the door, stop the phone,
Bend the time, early home.

And that's all there is to it! Give silent thanks to the oriades, profuse thanks to your boss and off you go!

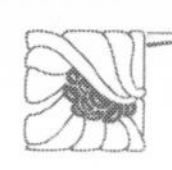

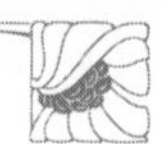

A spell to stand your ground

There are occasions in life when it pays to stand your ground. This can take some courage on your part, particularly if you are faced with adversity or hostility. So call on the mountain nymphs to help you stand strong and firm by using this spell.

You will need: Nothing.

Moon phase: Any – use whenever needed.

- All you need to do is speak the following charm:

Powers of the mountain nymphs I call,
Help me to stand strong and tall.
Standing firm and standing free,
My inner strength all shall see.
I call mountain nymphs from all around,
Help me now to stand my ground!

Whatever challenge you may face, know that you now have faerie strength to back you up.

Echo's spell for unrequited love

Having to endure unrequited love can be a harsh experience. It can be humiliating and damaging to your self-esteem – especially when the one you are emotionally attached to looks through you as though you are invisible! Read the tale of Echo to familiarise yourself with her story, and then try this little spell to ease the pain.

You will need: A piece of paper and a pen, your brewing pot or a heatproof dish.
Moon phase: Any.

- Go to your altar, cast the circle as described on pages 37–8 and light the illuminator candles.
- Write the name of the one you admire at the top of a sheet of paper. Beneath write out the following charm:

How much longer must I wait?
The game you play is cruel.
You reel me in just to pull away;
I grow tired of this duel.
I have loved you for so long,
Yet all you do is play,
Toy with my heart and pull its strings
Then cast it far away.
And so it's time to end this game
And heal this heart so sore,
Taking back my self-respect,
For I am worth much more!

- Fold the spell paper up, light it in one of the illuminator candles and allow it to burn in the brewing pot or heatproof dish.
- Take down the circle as described on page 38, give thanks to Echo and try to move on with your life.

Give something back ...

Once you have worked with the rock faeries, try to give something back in some way. For example, you could volunteer to help clean up a sacred site. Buy only one or two crystals of each variety – remember that the earth has to be invaded and mined with harmful explosives to extract these precious jewels, so don't buy dozens and dozens of them. There is no need to flaunt your lack of Wiccan wisdom in this way, as spells usually call for only one or two crystals at a time. Care for the earth – don't fund those who exploit her.

Petals

Petals of spring push through frozen earth,
Clothing the snowdrops which gave them their birth.
Heads drooping low, yet bringing good cheer,
For we know elementals of springtime are near.
Petals of summer will follow hard on,
As sunflowers turn and gaze after the sun.
Roses and lilies and bridal bouquets
Tell of the romance of long summer days.
Petals of autumn are leaves on the trees,
Falling from branches preparing to freeze,
Teaching the lesson all creatures must learn,
That all life to the earth must one day return.
Petals of winter are cheerful and merry,
The green of the pine and the red of the berry.
The earth cold and barren, yet life goes on still,
As the yule rose blooms despite winter's chill.
As all the bright seasons the earth passes through,
The wheel turns again to revive and renew.
Elementals of springtime, of summer and fall,
And the darkness of winter – we honour you all!

At the Bottom of the Garden ...

The idea of faeries living at the bottom of the garden is one that most of you will be familiar with. Many of you will have come across the concept of flower fairies during childhood. These elementals were made famous by Ciceley Mary Barker through her children's books of artwork and verse. But there is a magickal truth behind this popular image, for each flower has a life force and therefore an elemental.

These elemental faeries are known by different names in different parts of the world. In Germany, for instance, there are the moss maidens, healing faeries who are said to spin the blankets of moss that are found in parks, gardens, forests and woodlands. The vily are the Slavonic faeries of flowers and fruit, who have the ability to shapeshift into small animals and birds. In Poland these same elemental beings are called the willi. In Scandinavia a female faerie called the bil presides specifically over the witch's plant, henbane. This plant is deeply rooted in witchcraft and magickal folklore. It can be fatally poisonous when used incorrectly, so perhaps this is why it has been given its very own faerie guardian! In Hindu mythology, the elementals of trees and plants are collectively called dewas, from which word we derive the term deva, the English name for a nature spirit.

Blodeuwedd the flower maiden

In Celtic legend, Blodeuwedd was the most beautiful woman in the world. Her name means 'flower face' or 'born of flowers'. She was created by Gwydion, who made her from the blossoms of oak, broom and meadowsweet, and brought her to life using magick in order that she should become the wife of his nephew Lleu. This was duly accomplished, and for a time Blodeuwedd and Lleu lived in relative peace and harmony. Then, one day when Lleu was away, Blodeuwedd met Goronwy, who was hunting in the woods, and she fell instantly in love with him. Together they began to plot the murder of Lleu. Though their plans were carefully laid, Lleu shapeshifted into an eagle at the last moment and flew away, thus escaping death. When Gwydion heard of Blodeuwedd's betrayal he set out to avenge his nephew. He sought out Blodeuwedd and transformed her into an owl as punishment.

The tale of Blodeuwedd can teach us that we must always take responsibility for our own actions – and also that the grass isn't always greener on the other side! Blodeuwedd illustrates the fact that beauty isn't always synonymous with the fairest or truest heart and that we must look beneath the surface to the person within. In modern magick the owl has come to represent intellect and the wisdom that comes with a lesson learned, symbolism that may be rooted in the tale of Blodeuwedd.

Creating a Blodeuwedd thought form

The purpose of this thought form is similar to that of the banshee thought form on pages 62–3. However, while the banshee comes to warn you of impending disaster, Blodeuwedd will help you to come to terms with the consequences of your actions and so accept that life's toughest lessons are usually the ones from which you learn the most.

You will need: Nothing.
Moon phase: Any.

- Go to your altar, cast the circle as described on pages 37–8 and light the illuminator candles.
- Follow the basic instructions for creating a thought form on pages 31–3, adapting your visualisation to see a beautiful fresh-faced maiden with the bloom of the rose in her cheeks and eyes of cornflower blue. She has soft waves of hair that fall to her hips, and on her head is a pretty chaplet of fragrant blossom. In her hand she holds the feather of an owl.
- Breathe life into this thought form three times and then say the following charm to activate her powers:

Blodeuwedd of the flower face,
Help me meet my fate with grace.
By my actions I am bound
To accept the consequences that rebound.
My responsibilities I will not spurn,
For wisdom's lesson I will learn.

- In your mind's eye see Blodeuwedd offer you the wisdom of the owl's feather. Take this from her and then see her fade out in a shimmer of rainbow light. Know that you have invoked a powerful thought form who will help you to come to terms with your current challenge.
- To complete the magick, pick up the first feather you see after working this spell and keep it as a personal talisman of wisdom and a reminder of Blodeuwedd.

Flora

Flora is the Roman goddess of flowers and the season of spring. She is a particularly benign goddess, being gentle and nurturing in nature. She is queen of all the flower faeries, and the flowers are her gift to the earth. This is perhaps why people still give flowers and floral tributes to mark rites of passage such as birth, marriage, and death, and to celebrate occasions such as a birthdays and falling in love.

Indeed, some flowers have come to symbolise a particular event or occasion. Red roses, for example, are strongly associated with true love and symbolise a romantic attachment and regard. White lilies are popular in bridal bouquets and also in funeral wreaths – thus the lily has come to represent purity and the spirit. The red poppy is linked with loss and remembrance due to the significant role it plays on Remembrance Sunday, while the daffodil is the herald of spring. Aconite, deadly nightshade and hemlock are all linked with witches and witchcraft.

Buying flowers for your home is a great way to attune with this goddess and her hand maidens, the flower faeries.

Flora's secret spell

If you are giving flowers as a gift, work this spell to infuse them with your magick.

You will need: A bunch of flowers, some pretty wrapping paper and ribbons.

Moon phase: Any.

- Take your flowers to your altar and say:

I dedicate these flowers to the power and blessings of Flora.
So mote it be!

- Sit before your altar in silent meditation for a while and think about the person you will give the flowers to. Do they have any sadness or sorrow in their life at the moment? Are the flowers to be a gift for a celebration such as a birthday or recovery from illness?
- Take up a flower, hold it to your lips and breathe your love and good wishes into it five times. Do the same with each flower.
- Make the flowers into a pretty bunch and wrap them with the paper and ribbons, as you do so saying the following words:

Flora, Flora, goddess of blooms,
Weaving colour at the magickal loom,
I take these flowers to one I love
As a gift of magick from above.
As each pretty flower opens wide,
Let joy be felt from Flora's pride.

- Give the flowers to your loved one and know that as they blossom and open, they will release all your good wishes, hopes and dreams.

Flower power

In Victorian times the language of flowers was very popular. In this language all flowers had a secret and symbolic meaning, and giving a bouquet was often a way to pass on a private message. Today we can use the language of flowers in magick to tap into the symbolic meaning of flowers. For instance, should you require the gift of hope, you might attune with the faerie of the iris by surrounding yourself with these flowers and perhaps wearing a perfume containing essential oil of iris.

Essential oils are another wonderful tool for working with the flower faeries. You can attune with these elementals by burning essential oils in a burner or by mixing essential oils with an appropriate carrier oil and wearing them as perfume. Essential oils can also be used in your rituals, to anoint candles for example or to add flower power to a spell pouch or scattering powder. Simply visualise your chosen flower faerie as you work with the oil.

Each flower is associated with a different month, so to begin working with the flower faeries, you might like to choose the flower that is associated with your birth month, placing these blooms in a vase by your bed or on your desk or altar. Use the essential oil of your flower as often as you can. Alternatively, you might prefer to attune with a different flower faerie each month as the year rolls on. Below is a list of the flower faerie for each month and the areas she presides over.

Month	*Flower*	*Symbolising*
January	Narcissus	Self-love
February	Iris	Hope
March	Daffodil	Spring, chivalry
April	Daisy	Innocence, purity
May	Bluebell	Constancy
June	Rose	Love, feminine beauty
July	Cornflower	Delicacy, fragility
August	Dahlia	Dignity

September	Gladioli	Protection
October	Aster	Truth, honesty
November	Violet	Modesty, chastity
December	Carnation	Divinity

Toadstools and mushrooms

Toadstools and mushrooms have long been associated with faeries and faerie magick. The best-known of these is the fly agaric, a bright red mushroom with white spots. This type of mushroom has hallucinogenic properties and was used by Celtic priests and priestesses to induce a shamanic journey or vision quest. These hallucinogenic journeys could be the origin of tales of visits to faerieland! In Wiccan and Pagan tradition, mushrooms are used to represent and increase fertility, and it's easy to see why when you look closely at a mushroom, as they do have quite a phallic shape. There are lots of different mushrooms and some of them are poisonous, so you shouldn't pick them unless you can identify them accurately.

Mushrooms growing in a circle are known as a faerie ring. This is a sure sign of elemental activity. Tradition states that a faerie ring is a favourite place for faerie revels, when the faeries come out and dance in circles. Once again, there is a link here between folklore and magick, as witches often perform a circle dance in order to raise power for spells and rituals. Such dances usually take place in a meadow or forest, the better to commune with nature.

I took part in my first circle dance as an elf, at the age of eight – I was a member of the Brownie Guides! At the end of each Guide meeting we all joined hands and danced clockwise around a wooden fly agaric mushroom with a stuffed toy owl sitting on top, singing the Brownie Guide song as we went. If you were ever a Brownie, you will no doubt have had a similar experience! Years later, I can now see the pagan symbolism present in this simple childhood game: dancing clockwise and following the path of the sun; honouring an owl, a symbol of the Great Goddess; the wooden fly agaric mushroom, which is a symbol of the earth and the fey (I still have one of these standing in my hall!). Who would have thought that these old traditions would be kept alive by the predominantly Christian Girl Guide movement? It just goes to show that witchcraft never really died and that magick always finds a way!

The following two spells use mushrooms as a magickal tool. Make sure you use only safe mushrooms – buy them from a supermarket to be sure. Again, please don't pick wild mushrooms unless you are absolutely certain of your ability to identify them correctly!

A spell to keep someone in the dark

Mushrooms tend to grow in dark, shady places, so you can call on their powers if you need to keep someone in the dark for a while. Note that this spell should be used only for positive reasons, for example if you are planning a surprise party or birthday treat for someone. It should not be used to cover up any form of deceit or dishonesty. If you do use the spell for such purposes, you will eventually have to deal with the consequences, which could be quite nasty. You've been warned!

You will need: A plain garden mushroom.

Moon phase: Any.

- Take your mushroom and name it for the person you wish to be kept in the dark. Then whisper the reason for this (for example a surprise party).
- Place the mushroom at the back of a dark cupboard and leave it there until you have sprung your surprise.
- When your mission is accomplished, give the mushroom back to the earth by placing it in the garden. Finally, give your thanks to the fey.

A mushroom spell to enhance meditation

As we saw on page 139, certain species of mushroom were once used to induce shamanic visions and journeys. While ingesting mushrooms in this way is dangerous and not something you should experiment with, you can nevertheless use the magickal power of the mushroom to enhance your meditation in a much safer way.

You will need: 13 mushrooms.
Moon phase: Any.

- Use the mushrooms to make a circle on the floor, large enough to sit in. This is now your meditation space.
- Sit comfortably within this circle and say the following incantation three times:

Faeries of the magick ring,
Teach my soul how to sing.
Show me the vision, whisper the dream,
Guide me now to the realm of unseen.

- Now relax and begin your meditation, letting the fey lead your mind where they will.

The faerie dell

One of the best ways to attune with the flower faeries is to create a beautiful garden full of the flowers they most love. Even a balcony or a collection of window boxes can be filled with the plants and flowers that are best known for faerie activity, so if you don't have a garden you can still attune with the faeries in this way.

First clear your garden of anything that shouldn't be there, such as litter and broken garden furniture. Next begin to plant the flowers and trees that are closely associated with the faeries. Some ideas are: foxgloves, bluebells, brambles, dog rose, hawthorn, oak, holly, ash, buttercups, daisies and poppies.

To further encourage elemental activity, add garden ornaments of fairies and sprites and dot these around the garden too. Add bird baths and feeders to encourage wildlife. Then create a magickal faerie ring using decorative mushroom and toadstool ornaments (available from most garden centres). This will send a clear message to the fey that they are most welcome.

Set up a simple garden altar (see page 45) and place a traditional witches' broom by the back door of your house to invite the faerie elementals into your home. Finally, create a seating area in the garden. This will be your faerie arbour. This is a place where you can sit and think, commune with the fey and perhaps meditate outside.

Although a garden that has a faerie theme is great for any magickal practitioner, it is especially appropriate if you have small children – they will love the enchantment that fills your faerie dell.

Give something back ...

There are two main ways in which you can give back to the flower faerie elementals. Firstly, never pick wild flowers. Not only is it illegal but it also endangers the survival of certain species. Secondly, when you have flowers in the home, treat them with the respect they deserve. This means giving them clean water and attending to dead heads and leaves. Also, once the flowers begin to die and decay, please don't simply throw them in the bin! These flowers have given you pleasure and have brightened your home for several days, so honour them by placing them for a time in a special place, away from your altar, where you can allow them to begin to decay and decompose naturally. Then give thanks to the elementals for the pleasure the flowers have given you. Finally, give the flowers back to the earth by placing them in a corner of your garden.

Faerie Tale

Deep in the midst of a woodland glade,
Sleeping Beauty there is laid.
On a four-poster bed all covered with rose
In enchanted slumber she doth repose.
Not far away, a magickal tower
Stands within a faerie bower.
Imprisoned, Rapunzel holds on to hope
As she coils her hair into a rope.
As the clock starts to strike, Cinderella must flee;
She abandons the ball and the gay company,
Fleeing the palace as the twelfth stroke chimes,
Leaving the gift of a glass slipper behind.
Taking the path deep in the woods
Is a pretty young girl in a bright red hood,
Taking joy in her day, trusting all that she sees,
Never guessing a wolf hides in the trees.
As each pretty princess wanders the page,
She teaches a lesson that ripens with age.
Each tale has a message and a magickal core,
So invoke the enchantment and read them once more ...!

Once Upon a Time

No book of faerie magick would be complete without exploring the world of faerie tales, so in this chapter we are going to do just that. Faerie tales are stories that carry a moral lesson within them. They are a branch of mythology that most people are very familiar with and they have been used for centuries to teach youngsters about values, morals and codes of honour. However, it is only relatively recently that faerie tales have been viewed as a form of entertainment that is solely for children. And nothing could be further from the truth, for faerie tales have a wealth of symbolism hidden within them that is just as useful to adults as it is to children. In fact, faerie tales have been used as a psychological device to analyse the inner workings of the mind, most notably used by C G Jung.

To witches and magickal practitioners, faerie tales are a valuable source of reference. Hidden within each popular faerie tale is a core of magick and pagan symbolism. This shouldn't be too surprising, as most popular faerie tales have been in circulation in some form or another since the time of the Great Goddess, when the world revered a female deity. *Cinderella,* for example, had been passed down orally for many generations when it was finally written down for the first time in China during the ninth century. Although each faerie tale has been rewritten many times, and several versions of each may be in existence, the moral and magickal core of the story usually remains the same.

Faerie tales hold a key place in faerie magick, as they are the vehicle that first introduces us to the realm of the elementals. We can relate the lessons of each tale to our own lives, and we can take comfort and inspiration from the heroes and heroines they portray. Over the next few pages I am going to try to show you the magick within the world of faerie tales. Hopefully, you will come to see them in a completely new way.

The storyteller

In the past, storytelling was a highly regarded art form. This was especially so in Celtic and Druidic traditions. At the end of each day, families and clan would gather together around a huge fire, and great tales of heroes and adventure would be told. This was an oral tradition. Few could read or write, so stories had to be carefully memorised if they were to pass down through the generations. Out of this oral tradition came much of what we now know as the Norse sagas; Arthurian legend; Celtic, Greek and Roman myths; and, of course, the popular faerie tales we are all familiar with.

But what is it about stories that so intrigues us? And why were the old storytellers held in such high esteem? Perhaps it is because stories enable us to take a mental journey to far-off places and other worlds, enabling us to see our own world in a new and different way, and even to mentally become someone else for a while. It could also be because stories have the power to inspire us, and myths and legends to introduce us to the world of magick. In this sense, the storytellers themselves become the magicians.

Even today, bestselling authors can achieve a celebrity status and become household names. Think of writers such as Stephen King, J K Rowling, Terry Pratchett and Jilly Cooper. Such authors are our modern-day tribal storytellers, and society still places them in a position of honour.

Perhaps the best-known poets and storytellers of history were the great bards of the Druid tradition. Today's Druids still follow an oral tradition, learning and memorising their poems, sagas and rituals, largely without committing anything to paper.

In Wiccan tradition also, stories and poems are used in ritual and sabbat celebrations. Modern witches still make use of the tales of John Barleycorn and the Oak and Holly Kings in order better to understand the laws of nature and the passing of the seasons. Such stories have become part of the foundation of modern witchcraft. Poems and faerie tales can also be used in this way, helping us to understand ourselves and the world around us through symbolism, imagery and archetype. Such writings can also teach us more about the elementals, about magick in general and about the pagan Goddess.

La Belle Dame Sans Merci

'La Belle Dame Sans Merci' is the title of a poem by John Keats, one of England's great Romantic poets. The poem beautifully illustrates the inextricable link between the Goddess of magick and witchcraft and the maidens of faerie tale. It tells the tale of a knight who falls in love with a beautiful elven maid. This captivating faerie sings a spell song as she rides upon the besotted knight's horse. Then, leading him to her home, she feeds him honey and dew – both symbols of the divine feminine. This fey creature is actually a version of the pagan Goddess. She offers love and passion and enchants the poor knight with her Otherworldly charms. She is a symbol of love, inspiration, reckless desire, poetic vision, the season of spring, and ultimately the long sleep of death, for the knight eventually finds himself on the hillside 'so haggard and so woe begone'.

This is just one example of how faerie tale maids are thought to be derived from various aspects of the pagan Goddess. For those of you who are unfamiliar with this famous poem, here it is in its entirety:

La Belle Dame Sans Merci

O what can ail thee, knight at arms
Alone and palely loitering?
The sedge has wither'd from the lake,
And no birds sing.
O what can ail thee, knight at arms,
So haggard and so woe begone?
The squirrel's granary is full,
And the harvest's done.
I see a lily on thy brow,
With anguish moist and fever-dew,
And on thy cheeks a fading rose
Fast withereth too.
I met a lady in the meads,
Full beautiful, a faerie's child,
Her hair was long, her foot was light,
And her eyes were wild.
I made a garland for her head,
And bracelets too, and fragrant zone;
She look'd at me as she did love,
And made sweet moan.
I set her on my pacing steed,
And nothing else saw all day long,
For sidelong would she bend, and sing
A faery's song.

She found me roots of relish sweet,
And honey wild, and manna dew,
And sure in language strange she said –
'I love thee true'.
She took me to her elfin grot,
And there she wept and sigh'd full sore,
And there I shut her wild wild eyes,
With kisses four.
And there she lullèd me asleep
And there I dream'd – Ah! woe betide! –
The latest dream I ever dream'd
On the cold hill side.
I saw pale kings and princes too,
Pale warriors, death-pale were they all;
They cried – 'La Belle Dame Sans Merci
Hath thee in thrall!'
I saw their starved lips in the gloam,
With horrid warning gaped wide,
And I awoke and found me found me here,
On the cold hill's side.
And this is why I sojourn here
Alone and palely loitering,
Though the sedge is wither'd from the lake,
And no birds sing.

John Keats

Faerie tale magick

Faerie tales are rich in magickal symbols. The number three, for example, comes up time and time again: three sisters, three tasks, three kisses, three wishes and so on. In magickal terms the number three is linked to the Triple Goddess and her three aspects of Maiden, Mother and Crone. The ugly sister, wicked stepmother and evil faerie are also distorted versions of the Crone Goddess, the Dark Mother who teaches wisdom through life's lessons and spins out the web of fate. Meanwhile the heroine of the story begins as an innocent and naive maiden, but as the tale progresses, she endures a rite of passage in some form and so becomes the Mother aspect.

Magick mirrors are a more obvious magickal symbol. They are scrying vehicles in which visions of the past, present and future can be seen. Think of the magick mirror in *Snow White,* which cannot tell a lie. This mirror doesn't pander to the wicked queen's vanity – instead it tell her straight out that Snow White is 'far more fair than she'! This underlines a basic magickal truth – when you scry or use any form of divination, you may not get the answer you wanted!

Midnight, the witching hour, is also present in faerie tales, the most famous example being *Cinderella,* in which the clock chimes out the end of Cinderella's date with the handsome prince. As she flees from the ball and loses her glass slipper, Cinderella is suspended between two worlds, just as time is suspended for a moment between one day and the next. Cinderella's story could also have something to do with the female obsession with shoes!

At the heart of every faerie tale is a battle between good and evil, right and wrong, selflessness and selfishness. This illustrates the internal battle that goes on in most of us as we try to be pleasant, productive and responsible members of society. In psychology this inner darkness is known as our shadow self, and it is something we must all come to terms with. In magick we understand that the darkness has a place and a purpose, and we accept it as the polar opposite of light. In faerie tales this darkness must be confronted and faced before the heroine can move forward into the light and live happily ever after.

The princess and the prince

After overcoming all their trials and tribulations, the fair princess and the charming prince finally marry and the entire kingdom rejoices. This isn't just the stuff of faerie tales either – think back to the marriage of Prince Charles and Lady Diana Spencer, when the whole of the UK population went slightly mad at the idea that here was a real live, beautiful princess we could all adore and wave flags at! Wow ...! Deep down, people still want the faerie tale.

But if we look more closely at the role of the faerie tale princess and her prince, we can perceive an even older story – that of the divine female and her consort. The princess is always centre stage. Even when she isn't doing very much (for example, Sleeping Beauty or Rapunzel) she is still the main focus of the story. When things go wrong for her, the birds don't sing, the flowers droop and the natural world goes out on a sympathy strike!

Meanwhile the prince is hard at work, completing the tasks that have been set him and doing all he can to get to the right place at the right time, to be there when his princess needs him most. His is an active yet supporting role. He may not be the main character, but he is equally as important as our heroine. For without the prince, Sleeping Beauty and her world would slumber forever. And without Sleeping Beauty, the prince would have no goal and no purpose. Heroine and hero are inseparably connected, each depending on the existence of the other, yet each with a very different role to play. Thus the princess and the prince are simplified versions of the Goddess and the God. When they marry, the kingdom rejoices at this union of the divine feminine and masculine energies – the natural world grows and thrives and life goes on.

And you thought that faerie tales were just child's play! When it comes to magick, you must always look for the deeper meaning.

Are you a princess?

Are you the kind of girl who yearns for red roses, beautiful shoes that fit perfectly, diamond earrings or a four-poster bed? Do you long to ride in a horse-drawn carriage, dance till midnight and experience the magick of 'true love's first kiss'? Do you dream of a knight in shining armour galloping up on his feisty white steed to rescue you and sweep you away to a castle in the air? Does it send you dizzy with girlish glee when your man actually calls you Princess, My Lady, Fair Damsel and so on? Do you experience a full-on Ready Brek glow when he walks you to your side of the car and opens the door for you before he gets in himself? Or when he lifts your hand to his lips and kisses it? Or when he gives you his best cavalier-style bow? If so, you probably have a few 'princess issues'!

There is nothing wrong with this, but there are good princess issues and bad princess issues. I believe each and every woman has an inner princess just waiting to be acknowledged and recognised – but how you go about expressing her will determine whether you are Cinderella or one of the ugly sisters!

Good princess behaviour includes looking on the bright side, offering a helping hand to those who need it, being polite and well-mannered, keeping negative opinions to yourself, seeing the best in people, focusing on the positive aspects of any situation, and generally trying to improve yourself and be the best that you can be.

Bad princess behaviour includes bring rude and aloof, acting as if the world owes you a huge favour, treating people like servants who are there to do your every bidding, pouting and sulking when you don't get your own way, throwing a strop when things go wrong, expecting perfection from everyone and everything, running up debts and constantly living beyond your means, and generally having a bad attitude to people and to life.

No prizes for guessing which set of behaviours make for the nicer princess! In reality most of us have both good and bad princess traits. For instance, you may be a generally nice girl, but you just can't resist putting that pair of designer shoes on your credit card when you are already stretched to the limit financially. The trick is to learn to recognise when you are about to indulge in bad princess behaviour and replace it with a more positive action instead. Remember that in faerie tales the princess doesn't stamp her feet and scream when things go wrong – she quietly shoulders her burdens and makes the best of things, and for this positive attitude she is ultimately rewarded with a happy ending.

Having princess issues can also affect your romantic relationships in a number of ways, the most obvious being that if you are looking for the handsome prince or the white knight, you may experience several disappointments before you find him. There is a certain amount of truth in the saying 'You have to kiss a lot of frogs before you find your prince'! And such high expectations can be enough to frighten prospective suitors away, as they may be afraid they can't live up to your romantic ideals.

Now, I'm not saying that you should settle for second best in any way, but you do need to realise that your prince may be very different from the way you have envisioned him, so don't give your man the elbow just because he doesn't exactly fit the box you have created for him! The most important thing is how he treats you and if he truly loves you. One good test my friends and I have used to discover if a boyfriend could be our prince is to ask ourselves if we could see him in armour! If we can't even begin to imagine him filling the role of our romantic ideal, then maybe he's not the one. Of course, this test isn't foolproof, and you should get to know the man in question before you try it, but it's a good way to discover if you have a romantic attachment.

If the man in your life is your one true prince, you won't have to tell him that you need to be swept off your feet and treated like a fair princess – he will already have worked this out for himself because he's recognised and acknowledged your inner princess and he wants to woo her! Red roses, chocolates, diamond earrings and expensive perfumes should be things he surprises you with, not things you command or expect from him. Allow him to indulge his own inner prince and woo you without taking advantage of his kind nature and generous spirit. And if, like Julia Roberts in the film *Pretty Woman*, you want the faerie tale, then be prepared, because there may come a day when your prince needs you to rescue him right back!

Which princess are you?

What's your favourite faerie tale? Maybe you have more than one. Maybe you haven't thought about it in such a long time that you've completely forgotten which story you loved as a child. If so, think about it now. Reread the old tales and rediscover your favourite, for this story will have a special meaning for you and will determine which kind of princess you are and what particular life skill you may be here to learn. Let's take a look at the most popular faerie tales and consider their magickal significance to the witch, beginning with one of my personal favourites, *Sleeping Beauty*.

Sleeping Beauty

Sleeping Beauty is one of the most popular and well-loved faerie tales. Almost all of us are familiar with the story of the beautiful maiden cursed by a wicked faerie and doomed to prick her finger on an enchanted spindle and sleep for 100 years. Only true love's first kiss has the power to awaken her, and only if this happens at the appointed time. As Beauty lies sleeping on a four-poster bed, surrounded by fragrant roses, the rest of the kingdom and the land sleep with her, until the arrival of the Prince, when his kiss breaks the spell.

In terms of magick, this is a tale about being reborn, and its key word is initiation. Young Beauty goes happily through life until her

15th year, when she comes across an old lady spinning. This old lady is a symbol of the Crone, or Dark Mother, who presides over destiny and spins the web of fate. Thus Beauty meets her fate and pricks her finger on the spindle, falling into her enchanted sleep. This is where her initiation begins, for she falls asleep as a child and will awaken as a young woman ready for love and the responsibilities of adulthood.

If *Sleeping Beauty* is your favourite faerie tale, your life path will include some form of initiation, as that is the lesson you are here to learn. This initiation could be of a spiritual nature, such as the kind taken in witchcraft, or it could be a life-changing experience such as motherhood, surviving an illness or injury, or being reborn after or because of a significant relationship in your life. However this initiation happens, it will be for your highest good and will leave you feeling as if you've just come out of a deep sleep.

To attune with your inner Sleeping Beauty, say the following incantation three times whenever you need her magick:

As Sleeping Beauty does repose
Beneath the fragrant summer rose,
So I have lived in sleeping state
But will wake up now and embrace my fate.
Initiated I will be
Into a brand new destiny!

Cinderella

Cinderella is probably the best loved faerie tale of all, and it is certainly among my favourites. It tells the story of a young maid who is treated horribly by her stepmother and two stepsisters. She is forced to cook and clean for them and is little more than a downtrodden servant. That is until her faerie godmother shows up and transforms Cinders into the belle of the ball, enabling her to capture the heart of the charming prince with her gentleness, modesty and beauty. But, of course, faerie tale magick only lasts until midnight, at which time Cinderella must flee, or the Prince will discover she is but a servant girl dressed in rags. Flee she does, leaving behind one of her beautiful glass slippers. The charming prince scours the country with this slipper, vowing to marry the one it fits, for she must surely be the mysterious girl from the ball. Eventually, he finds Cinderella and places the glass slipper on her tiny foot. Of course, it fits perfectly, and so he takes her to his palace to be his royal princess.

It is the original rags-to-riches story, but more than that, *Cinderella* is a tale of transcendence, with the faerie godmother being the Goddess in disguise, offering the chance of a new life. Only after much trial and tribulation can Cinders move into her new role as the princess and live happily ever after. Only after being treated badly does she experience the heady delights of true love, respect and adoration.

If *Cinderella* is your favourite faerie tale, your life path will include some form of transcendence. However, this also means that you will probably have to face some form of challenge or struggle in life before your transcendence can take place. If your life often seems to be a series of unfortunate events, take heart from your faerie tale heroine and know that things will get better and you will eventually find your true role in life.

To attune with your inner Cinderella, say the following incantation three times whenever you need her magick:

As Cinderella flees the ball,
I vow to give my life my all.
I'll wear my rags with Cinders' pride
Till my true role in life I find.
I'll take all knocks that life sends
And through the struggle I will transcend!

Beauty and the Beast

Beauty and the Beast is a wonderful love story. Beauty is the youngest of four motherless daughters. Her father dotes on her because, unlike her sisters, Beauty is kind, generous, helpful and unselfish. When Beauty's father has to go away for a while, he asks his daughters what present they would like him to bring back for them. While her sisters ask for expensive gowns and jewels, Beauty asks for a single white rose. This rose is a symbol of her innocence and purity. So her father sets off on his travels, and on his way home he sees a beautiful garden of white roses. He slips into the garden and stealthily plucks the most beautiful white rose growing there.

At that moment a fearsome beast pounces out at him and declares that he must die as punishment for stealing the rose. The beast allows the man to return to his daughters to bestow his final gifts on them, but makes him promise to return in three months' time. Beauty, of course, is distraught at hearing of her father's fate, and when the three months is up, she steals off to take her father's punishment upon herself.

Thus Beauty and the beast finally meet, and although at first she is terrified of the fearsome creature, she eventually comes to see the gentle, kind-hearted being he is underneath. Eventually, she realises that the beast has no intention of killing her and she begs to go and visit her family. The beast agrees, but makes Beauty promise to return in a week. However, when beauty returns home, she finds that her father is ill, and it takes longer than a week to nurse him back to health. Thus, on her return to the beast, she discovers that he is dying of heartbreak and misery without her. It is at that moment that Beauty confesses her great love for the beast, and as she does so he turns into a handsome prince. He tells Beauty that her love for him has broken the spell that an evil enchantress put upon him some years before, condemning him to go through life as a hideous beast. Of course, in the end Beauty and the beast/prince marry and live happily ever after.

This story is ultimately about judgement and the false assumptions we make based on someone's appearance, career and material possessions. If this is your favourite faerie tale, you may find yourself 'keeping up with the Joneses' in an effort to create the right impression. You may be quite judgemental of others, but you judge yourself even more harshly. You may even hide behind an outlandish image in order to conceal your self-perceived shortcomings. Try to remember the deeper meaning of your favourite faerie tale and make an effort to let yourself and others off the hook. Remember the value of unconditional love, and love people for who they are, not what they are.

To attune with your inner Beauty, say the following incantation three times whenever you need its magick:

Beauty with your rose of white,
Help me look beyond first sight.
Beneath appearance I would see
To the person underneath.
My judgements I will set aside
And see the beauty deep inside.

Rapunzel

Most of you will be familiar with this tale of the beautiful princess held prisoner inside her ivory tower by a wicked witch. Rapunzel was the fairest maid in the land, but her great beauty was hidden from view, locked away in a tower with no door or staircase, only a window high up at the top of the turret. When the witch wished to visit Rapunzel, she would tell her to let down her beautiful long golden hair, which the witch would use as a rope to climb up into the tower chamber.

Rapunzel had a beautiful voice and she would sing songs to while away the hours. One day a prince was riding through the woods and became enchanted by Rapunzel's singing. Finding the tower, he soon discovered that there was no way in, so he sat beneath a tree to try to work out a way to get inside. It was at this moment that he heard the old witch shout 'Rapunzel, Rapunzel! Let down your hair!' and, watching through the trees, he saw her climb up the tower using Rapunzel's hair as a rope. Waiting until the witch had gone, the prince made himself known to Rapunzel and asked her to let down her hair. Then he climbed into the tower, where they made plans for Rapunzel's escape. However, the witch discovered these plans, cut off Rapunzel's hair and cast the prince from the window. He landed in a blackthorn bush and was blinded by the thorns.

Rapunzel and the prince both lived unhappily apart for several years, until the old witch died and Rapunzel was free. She searched for the prince and when she found him blind, she cried for his pain and suffering. As Rapunzel's tears touched the prince's eyes, his sight returned and he was completely healed. The lovers then went on to build a happy life together.

Rapunzel is a story of careful timing and its key word is 'retreat'. Only when the time is right does Rapunzel finally escape the enchanted tower. And only when the time is right does she find her prince. Once again, the wicked witch is a distorted version of the Crone Goddess, presiding over fate and teaching that sometimes the wisest action is to do nothing.

If this is your favourite faerie tale, your life path will probably include some form of retreat. This could mean that you are a naturally self-contained person who enjoys their own company. Or it could mean that you often go on a spiritual or religious retreat. Maybe you have a second home or a private room in your house that serves as a retreat. Whatever form your retreat takes, it is important to you to have your own space – and you may even have been inspired to turn your home into something of an ivory tower!

Healing is also likely to be an aspect of your life, whether you are involved in the nursing profession or simply in helping friends and loved ones through difficult times. Maybe you often find yourself taking on the role of counsellor within your circle of friends. Nevertheless, it is important to you to preserve your own time and space for yourself, in addition to helping others when you can.

To attune with your inner Rapunzel, say the following incantation three times whenever you need her magick:

Rapunzel with your hair so long,
In my tower I know I'm strong.
Safe and sound, I bide my time
And wait until I've had a sign.
Then I'll venture forth into life
And use my gifts to heal strife.

The Snow Queen

The Snow Queen is the Winter goddess, and in this story she has gone against her sisters, Spring, Summer and Autumn, to make the world forever winter. However, she is not the true heroine of the tale. This is a young girl called Gerda, who is in love with a boy called Kai. Magickally speaking, the Snow Queen represents the female icon of temptress, while Gerda represents the virgin. In the tale, the Snow Queen steals Kai away to her winter palace, where she gives him the task of mending her magick mirror, which has shattered into a thousand pieces. Meanwhile brave Gerda must make an epic journey through the seasons in order to reach the Snow Queen's winter palace and rescue her true love, Kai. It's interesting that in this tale it is the girl who must rescue the boy, thus proving her love for him, rather than the other way around, as is more usual. But only Gerda has the power to defeat the Snow Queen. Once Gerda has rescued Kai, who has meanwhile fixed the mirror, the long winter passes and the seasons all fall into place again.

This faerie tale is about the battle that goes on in each woman between the inner archetypes of virgin and temptress. Only when a long journey has been taken can these two archetypes come to terms with one another and coexist together, taking their rightful place without conflict. Thus the key word for the Snow Queen is 'journey', and if this is your favourite faerie tale, your life path will include some form of epic journey. This could be a literal journey, in that you choose to travel the world, or it might be a spiritual journey, or a symbolic journey following an illness or traumatic event. It might even be a similar kind of journey to the one in the story, in which you must do battle to come to terms with both your virgin and your temptress traits. Think about who you most relate to as you read the story. Are you totally on Gerda's side or do you have strong sympathies with the Snow Queen, who merely wants the world to see and appreciate the beauty of the winters she creates.

To invoke the magick of this faerie tale into your life, say the following incantation three times:

Snow Queen with your temptress ways,
Bringing cold and frosty days,
Help people see my unique grace
So I may take my given place,
Making way for the spring
That my heart may warm to all it brings.

Little Red Riding Hood

The story of Little Red Riding Hood is an old one. Red Riding Hood is sent to visit her sick grandmother, taking with her a basket of cakes and wine. To get from the village where she lives to her grandmother's cottage, Red Riding Hood must walk through the woods. She is given strict instructions not to stray from the path and not to speak to strangers, but on the way through the forest she meets a wolf and strikes up a conversation with him. Before long, she has told the wolf where her grandmother lives and the purpose of her errand. The wolf suggests that Red Riding Hood pick a bunch of wild flowers for her grandmother to help cheer her up. And so Red Riding Hood strays from the path and picks flowers.

Meanwhile the wolf goes straight to grandmother's cottage, eats grandmother up and then, dressed in her clothes, climbs into bed to wait for Red Riding Hood to arrive. Arrive she does, and doesn't see through the wolf's disguise until it is too late and he pounces on her and eats her up! Afterwards the wolf falls fast asleep, but his loud snoring alerts the woodcutter. Seeing the wolf, he raises his axe and cuts open the wolf, killing him and freeing Red Riding Hood and her grandmother. Red Riding Hood never strays from the path again!

This is a tale about a lesson learned, and its key word is 'trust'. It simply doesn't occur to Red Riding Hood not to trust the wolf. Danger is all around her, yet she still trusts all that she sees. By the end of the story, however, she has learned her lesson and knows that it pays to follow her mother's advice and not stray from the path or talk to strangers! She is wiser and more guarded, and so takes responsibility for her own safety.

If this is your favourite faerie tale, you have some kind of lesson to learn about trust. Maybe you need to learn to trust your instincts more and become more guarded. Perhaps you have trusted the wrong people in the past and this has led you into a dangerous situation or open to deception, trickery and betrayal. Try to be more aware of your surroundings and take responsibility for your own safety.

To attune with your inner Red Riding Hood, say the following incantation three times whenever you need its magick:

As Little Red Riding Hood walks through the woods,
I ask for the wisdom to know who to trust.
When danger appears I will remain calm
And rely on myself to keep me from harm.
My lesson I've learned and now I can see
Where the wild wolf hides under the trees.

A faerie godmother spell to grant a boon

Before you work this spell, make sure that the boon you wish to have granted is the true desire of your heart.

You will need: A silver candle in a suitable holder, some matches or a lighter.

Moon phase: Any.

- Light the candle, close your eyes and visualise your own faerie godmother standing before you. Her wings are large and sparkly, and her wand is upraised ready to grant your boon.
- When you can see your faerie godmother clearly, recite the following charm three times:

Faerie godmother, wand held high,
Keeper of my dreams,
I acknowledge your presence within my life,
For nothing is what it seems.
Fiction, fable, myth and legend –
But I see through your disguise.
Magick did not with childhood end;
The Goddess stands before my eyes.
Shining starlight in your wings,
Your gown shimmers like the moon.
Join me in my magickal ring;
Fey-mother, grant my boon!

- Make your wish, blowing out the candle as you do so. Save the candle to repeat the spell for future boons. Spend the rest of the day doing something 'fey' – read faerie tales or work some of the spells in this book. Watch out for signs that your faerie godmother has granted your wish and thank her when your spell manifests.

Turn your life into a faerie tale

I hope that this chapter has made you look at the world of faerie tales in a more magickal way. To witches, each faerie tale has a deep meaning, and we use its teaching to help us improve our lives. If your favourite faerie tale doesn't appear in this chapter, then try to find its key word and message yourself, then write a charm to suit, using the ones in this chapter as a guide.

To bring even more faerie tale magick into your life, buy a book of fables and read one every day, seeing the magickal wisdom they contain. Look for aspects of the pagan Goddess within the tales and attune with her via these stories.

Also try to bring the essence of faerie tales into your home and surroundings. Grow deep-red roses up the walls of your house, invest in a four-poster bed, buy ornaments that have their foundation in faerie tale such as a glass slipper, a red apple made of wood or glass, a crystal rose, wall sconces fashioned to look like briar roses and designed to hold tea-lights, a red velvet cloak, a pair of silver shoes or ruby slippers, a tiara, an ornate mirror and so on. Fill your life with representations of faerie tale magick, and your life in turn will become something of a faerie tale!

How to live happily ever after ...

Happiness is largely a question of attitude. While all of us have bad days, trials and personal challenges to come to terms with, the trick to living happily ever after is to maintain a positive outlook on life. Tell yourself that even the dark times will eventually pass and you can look forward to happy days of sunshine and birdsong! In the meantime, work on setting positive goals and creating a life map for yourself so you know where you're going.

Begin to live happily ever after from today by finding one thing each day to be happy about! This needn't be a big thing – a beautiful sunset, a surprise compliment, a text from a friend, an unexpected windfall and so on. Just find one thing at the end of each day to be happy about. In time you will end each day with a whole list of positive events and you will realise that you are indeed living happily ever after!

Morgana Enchants Accalon

Welcome to my world,
Where witches dance and dragons dwell.
Welcome to my world,
Where love is summoned by power of spell.
Welcome to the Enchanted Realm,
Where clocks tick on yet time stands still.
Welcome to the faerie realm,
Though you are not in Hollow Hill.
Welcome, my most honoured guest.
Pray, step into the keep.
Cast off your armour, take your rest
And dream this dream of waking sleep.

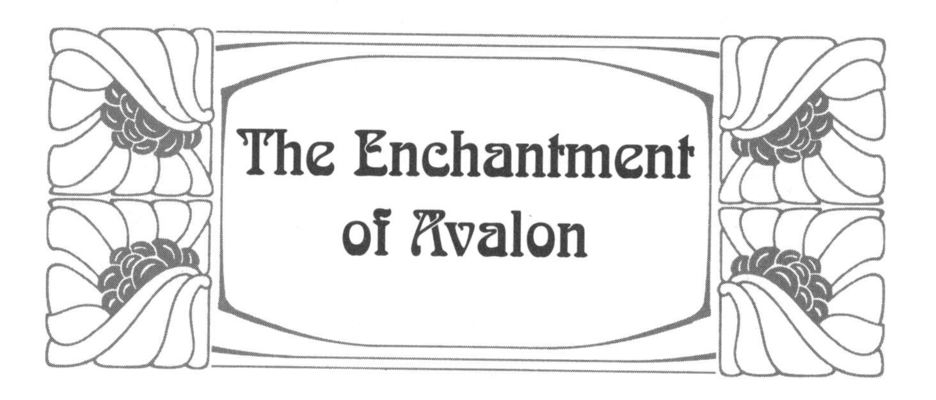

The Enchantment of Avalon

We have already see that faeries and elemental beings exist on the astral plane and that this plane is often referred to as the Otherworld. There are many versions of the Otherworld. In Irish tradition it is called the land of Tir na nOg, in Welsh legend it is the realm of Annwn. To the ancient Greeks it was called Elysium, while to many modern witches and Druids it is known as the Summerland. But by far the best-known version of the Otherworld is the isle of Avalon, a mysterious place of magick and enchantment, inhabited by fey maids and women such as Morgan le Fey, Tryamour, Argante and, of course, the Lady of the Lake, Vivienne.

So strong is the fascination with Camelot and Avalon that some covens and solitary witches choose to follow an Avalonian tradition, using Arthurian legend as a foundation for their magick and rituals. Indeed, most witches tend to view King Arthur and his Queen, Guinevere, as aspects of the pagan God and Goddess. And there is no doubt that Arthurian folklore is bursting with magick and elementals! If you have an affinity with these characters and archetypes, then this chapter will be of particular interest to you, for here we will be looking at Avalonian magick and the faerie maidens who inhabit this sacred island.

Avalon – the Isle of Apples

Avalon is an Otherworldly island that lies to the west of Camelot. It is a place of great peace and beauty, where the ill and the wounded are restored and the dead find their final resting place and an enchanted afterlife. The ladies of Avalon reside in a beautiful palace where every luxury is available to them, and yet they remain generous and unspoilt. Faeries and elemental beings pass between this enchanted Otherworld and our own world – thus the Lady of the Lake is on hand to give Arthur the magickal sword Excalibur, and both she and Morgan le Fey are frequent visitors to the court of Camelot. A magickal mist known as the Dragon's Breath keeps Avalon hidden from mortal view, although should a sudden fog appear in our world it is said to be a sure sign that an entrance to Avalon is close by!

The idea of the Otherworld being an island in the west is an old one. This is the direction of the setting sun and so it is naturally associated with rest, sleep and death. That a stretch of water must be crossed to get to Avalon is indicative of dream magick and visions, as Water is the element associated with all dreams, divinations and intuition. This is echoed in the way the ladies of Avalon use various scrying tools, such as magick mirrors and pools of water, to keep themselves informed of life at Camelot and the wider world around them. They may be quite isolated on their magickal island but they make use of their magick to keep in touch with what's going on in the world and to see visions of the future.

Avalon is also known as the Isle of Apples. This further supports the idea that the Arthurian tales are connected with the Great Goddess, as the apple is a symbol of the divine feminine and is sacred to her. The palace of Avalon is also said to be surrounded by beautiful apple orchards, and the name Avalon could have come from various Celtic words meaning 'apple' – the Breton *avallen,* the Welsh *afall* or the Celtic *avallo.* Apples are also considered to be the fruit of the faeries, and they are said to bestow wisdom, knowledge, youth, beauty and even immortality on the one who eats them.

The Avalonian Great Rite

In Wicca, the Great Rite is the symbolic union of masculine and feminine energies. This is usually achieved by plunging the athame (masculine) into the chalice (feminine), thus illustrating the divine union of energies from which all life stems. In Avalonian magick, this traditional rite is given a different twist and the athame is plunged into the heart of an apple, following the line of the core. You can incorporate this simple ritual into any of the spells in this chapter.

You will need: An athame (this is one of the few instances in faerie magick where it is permissible to use a traditional metal athame), an apple, a chopping board or other non-slip protective surface.
Moon phase: Any.

- Place the apple on the chopping board and say:

  This apple of Avalon represents the divine feminine.

- Hold the athame in both hands and carefully push the blade into the apple from the stem downwards. As you do so say:

  By all the powers of Avalon, I perform this Great Rite.
  May my magick give birth to my dreams. So mote it be!

- Gently remove the athame from the apple and at the end of your spellwork place the apple outside in your garden or another green place. You have now performed the Avalonian Great Rite.

Conjuring the Dragon's Breath

There are occasions in life when we may want to keep something from the prying eyes of others. This could be a secret item such as a birthday gift for a loved one, or it could be yourself, on an occasion when you feel the need to move swiftly through a crowd unnoticed. You may just have a wish for more privacy in general. This little ritual can help you in all of these things. All you need is your powers of visualisation and concentration.

You will need: Nothing.
Moon phase: Any.

- Go to a quiet place and breathe deeply for a few moments, until you feel centred.
- Focus on what you wish to hide. Maintain a picture of this in your mind and then visualise a thick fog swirling around and obscuring the item, as you do so speaking the following incantation and continuing for as long as your visualisation remains clear and focused:

I conjure up the Dragon's Breath
And swathe my secret in foggy folds.
From prying eyes and seeking minds
The Dragon's Breath my secret holds.
So mote it be!

The spell is now complete.

The tale of Tryamour

The tale of Tryamour is a little-known corner of Arthurian legend. Tryamour was a beautiful faerie maid who met and fell in love with Launfal, a knight of King Arthur's Round Table. Her name means 'test of love'. Tryamour and Launfal made an agreement that she would appear at his request on the condition that he would summon her only when he was entirely alone and would never speak of her and their great love for one another to anyone else.

They went on in this way quite happily for a time, until the handsome Launfal caught the Queen's eye! Launfal rejected Queen Guinevere's attentions, and when she flew into a rage, he angrily replied that he was deeply in love with one far more beautiful than the Queen. In this brief loss of temper, Launfal had not only caused deep offence to his queen but broken his promise to his true love, Tryamour.

In revenge for this insult, Guinevere arranged to have Launfal put on trial, and when he told his tale, he was commanded to produce his faerie lover within one year or be put to death. However, Tryamour would no longer appear at Launfal's summons, for he had broken his promise. When the year was up, Launfal stood in the courtyard of Camelot, bravely awaiting his fate. Just then a strange mist descended. Through the mist came Tryamour, her long hair flying out behind her as she galloped up on an exquisite white unicorn. His honour restored, Launfal mounted up behind Tryamour and the two lovers rode off to the Otherworld of Avalon, where they lived happily ever after.

The test of love spell

Just as Launfal and Tryamour's love is tested by outside influences (Guinevere), so most couples eventually have to endure some form of test, in which the strength of their love is put on trial. This test could take the form of financial pressures, work commitments, interfering family members or any one of a number of other things. If you find yourself in this situation, try working this little spell to help you and your partner over the bumps in the road.

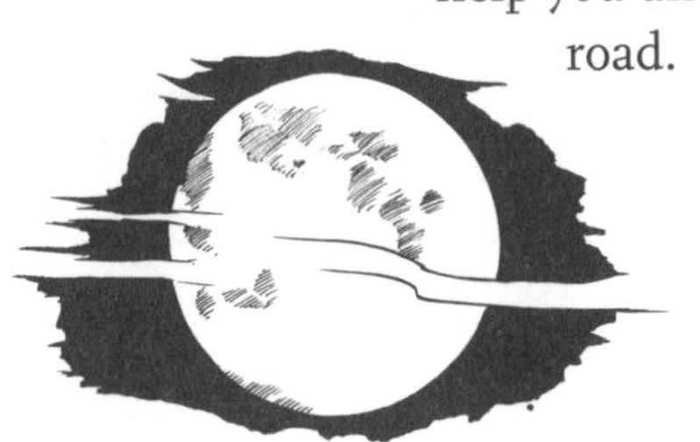

You will need: A silver candle and holder, a photo of you and your partner, a few rose petals.
Moon phase: Any – this is an emergency spell, so perform it whenever you need it.

- Take all that you need to a quiet corner of your bedroom. Place the photo on a sturdy surface in front of you (a bedroom altar is ideal) and the silver candle, in the holder, in front of the photo. Scatter the rose petals around both the candle and the photo.
- Take a few deep breaths to centre yourself. Gaze into the candle flame and say:

  I call on the strength and magick of the faerie maid Tryamour. My lover and I face a test of love. Please guide and support me through this difficult time and help me to remember that true love can conquer all. I give thanks for your aid and support, Tryamour. Blessed be!

- Remain at your altar for a while longer, then when you feel ready blow out the candle and go about your day. Light the candle again for a few minutes whenever you feel the need of extra strength and support for your relationship.

The Lady of the Lake

The Lady of the Lake is a key figure in Arthurian legend and Avalonian magick. She is known by the names of Vivienne, Nimue and Niniane, and she is said in some versions of the tales to be the Queen of Avalon – in other versions this role is given to Morgan le Fey or to the faerie maid Argante. The Lady of the Lake is a powerful sorceress and it is she who brings up Lancelot, giving him the name Lancelot du Lac and preparing him for his role as the greatest knight of the Round Table. As the Queen of Avalon, she teaches Morgan le Fey the secrets of magick and spellcasting, for it is Morgan who will eventually become the next Avalonian queen and high priestess. Vivienne is also a healer and prophetess and, being a Water elemental, she understands that all things must change. She uses her powers for the greater good of all. It is Vivienne who entombs the wizard Merlin with his own magick when he becomes too hungry for power.

Of course, the Lady of the Lake is best known for being the keeper of the great sword Excalibur, and it is her hand that rises from the lake to catch this sword on Arthur's death. She is also one of the three queens, along with Guinevere and Morgan le Fey, who ride the barge that takes Arthur into the Otherworld of Avalon, where he waits to be reborn at the hour when England needs him most. Thus the Lady of the Lake is also the guardian of the 'once and future king'.

The Lady of the Lake is associated with precognitive dreaming, divinations, scrying and prophecy, and her wisdom can be called upon to guide you to your ultimate destiny. To attune with her, scry in mirrors and pools of water, visit lakes and lochs as often as you can and spend time looking out over the water's surface. This is especially magickal if you and a loved one take a picnic and sit by the lake at full moon. Alternatively, bring Vivienne's energies into your home by working the following simple spell.

A Lady of the Lake spell

For this spell you will need to find a poster or art card depicting the Lady of the Lake. Reproductions by many New Age artists are available. Look out for the works of Jack Shalatain, Keith English, Linda Garland and Briar.

You will need: A picture of the Lady of the Lake and a frame suitable for hanging it, some spring water.
Moon Phase: Full.

- Place the picture in the frame and dab each corner of the frame with a drop of the spring water, as you do so saying:

  I bless this picture with the powers of Water. It now represents the magickal energies of Vivienne, the Lady of the Lake. So mote it be!

- Hang the picture on the wall, close to your bed, where you can see it as you fall asleep. Now say:

  May the blessings, guidance and wisdom of the Lady of the Lake come to me in my dreams. This is my will. So mote it be!

Your spell is complete. Remember to take special note of all your dreams from now on, perhaps writing them down in a dream journal.

Morgan le Fey

Morgan le Fey is probably the best-known resident of Avalon. She is also much maligned and misunderstood. Her name means Morgan the Faerie, thus illustrating her fey origins. Although she is often portrayed as evil, this is largely due to the old legends being radically changed and rewritten by early members of the Christian church. Eventually, the pagan symbolism of the legends was completely Christianised, and the powerful pagan priestess and eventual Queen of Avalon, Morgan, became an evil schemer plotting the downfall of her brother, the King.

Most versions of the legends say that Morgan le Fey is the King's half-sister. In paganism, King Arthur is viewed as an aspect of the Sun God, with Morgan taking on the role of Queen of Winter. This links her to the Celtic faerie goddess the Cailleach Bheur, the blue hag of winter, who brings in the darker days and the frosts and snows.

Morgan le Fey is a mistress of magick and sorcery. She is a skilled midwife and herbalist, knowing the plants that can kill and cure. She divines the future and summons the fogs and winds, including the magickal Dragon's Breath (see page 170). She has the ability to shapeshift into any animal, but frequently chooses the form of a rook or crow. This enables her to travel forth from Avalon and to see without being seen and recognised. The crow also links her to the ancient Celtic triple goddess the Morrigan – indeed, it is quite possible that the mythological Morgan le Fey is derived from this battle goddess of war.

The name Morgan means 'born of the sea', and Morgan le Fey is almost certainly related to the Lady of the Lake and to the sirens known as Morgens or Marie Morganas (see pages 90–1). Indeed, in some versions of the legends, she is called Morgana Le Fey. This connection also ties in with Morgan le Fey's enchanting allure and seductive charm, which she uses to enamour Accolon, one of Arthur's truest knights, and so remain informed of life at Camelot.

In Avalonian magick, Morgan le Fey is viewed as the main

archetypal goddess, and rituals are often performed in her name. As a faerie companion and elemental, she can assist you with divinations and can guide you on the magickal path. To attune with her, light a purple candle, focus on the flame and speak the following incantation nine times:

Morgan le Fey, born of the sea,
Bring out the magick and enchantment in me.
Teach me the power of darkness and light;
Help me become a Queen of the Night.
Smiling, beguiling, ensnaring them all,
By magick and spell I hold them in thrall!

Repeat the incantation whenever you need an extra boost to your magick, calling on Morgan le Fey to assist and guide you.

Queen Guinevere

Guinevere, whose name means 'white spirit', is a sovereign goddess of the land. Some schools of thought suggest that she is derived from the Welsh goddess Gwenhidw, or even from Blodeuwedd (see page 134). She is certainly of fey origin, and this is indicated in several ways. Firstly, Guinevere marries King Arthur at Beltane. Not only is this the favoured time for faerie weddings but it is also the time when the King and the land must consummate their union. In some versions of the story this is via Arthur's marriage to Guinevere, but in others it occurs when he mistakenly sleeps with Morgan le Fey, the high priestess of Avalon.

Guinevere is at first happily married to Arthur and the kingdom thrives. But then Lancelot comes along and upsets the apple cart! When the king discovers his wife's infidelity and betrayal, both he and the kingdom are plunged into a great depression. Only when Arthur's Queen is happy is the land joyous and fruitful, again illustrating Guinevere's role as goddess.

At Arthur's death, Guinevere takes her place beside him on the great barge as one of the three queens (i.e. the Triple Goddess), and together they go into the west and so to Avalon. Although in later Christianised versions of the legends Guinevere joins a convent or is burnt at the stake for her affair with Lancelot, in the earlier tales she resides in Avalon after Arthur's death.

Guinevere is a love goddess. She is a symbol of female independence and freedom of spirit, and, like Helen of Troy, she will always be regarded as a femme fatale! She can assist you in holding your personal space and maintaining your independence, and she can also help you better to understand the land. To attune with Guinevere, light a white candle and say the following incantation nine times:

Guinevere, white spirit, lady of the land,
I'll maintain my independence and learn to make a stand.
Help me trust my instincts and set my spirit free.
I call on your loving guidance. So mote it be!

Repeat the incantation whenever you feel that your freedom or independence is being compromised.

Moving on ...

Many books are available on the subject of Arthurian legend and Avalonian magick, so I do hope that you will continue to study this subject. Remember to look for the magickal symbolism and use the legends as a foundation for writing your own spells. And if you can, try to visit places that have an Arthurian link, such as Glastonbury, Tintagel and Carmarthen. This is a great way to attune with the faerie elementals of the legends. Glastonbury in particular has long been linked with Avalon. Learn as much as you can and then use your new-found knowledge in your magick.

Beings of Light

They dance in the starlight and speak through your dreams,
They twirl through the galaxy and surf the moonbeams.
Where angels have stood a peace lingers on,
And when they pass by, all sorrow is gone.
The ringing of bells is their voice as they sing;
In a flurry of snow they spread out their wings.
The breath of the wind is an angel in flight,
And watching over your soul is a being of light.
When life knocks you hard and you're filled with despair,
They teach you to hope and show you they care.
They take away pain and they calm all your fear;
When silence descends, you know one is near.
And they send a white feather as a celestial sign
That the angels are with you and they want you to shine!

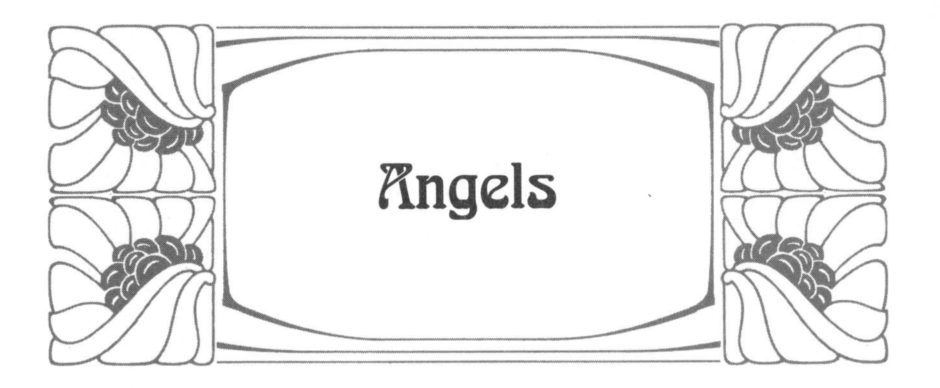

Angels

What better way to end a book of elemental magick than with the highest elementals of all – the angels. Angels are celestial beings of light and love, and they serve as a link between ourselves and the divine. They are a part of all cultures and religions. In mythology they appear as the Roman lares and the Norse valkyries. They are strongly associated with both the Christian and the Jewish faith, but anyone can work with angels, regardless of their religious beliefs.

Angels are ever present and will always answer a sincere call for help. Bringing their energies into your life can increase your sense of joy and well-being, fill your life with peace and love, and help you through a troubled time. Many people have had angelic experiences, ranging from a deep feeling of peace and love, to a sense of being protected, to actual angel sightings. There are lots of books available that relate such experiences, and they make for fascinating reading. In the meantime, this chapter will serve as a basic introduction to the angelic realms and the art of angel magick.

Angels and magick

Like all the other elementals we have looked at so far, angels can be called upon to assist you in your magickal rituals. They are messengers of love and can serve as a magickal link between you and your loved ones, thus aiding positive communication. When the angels are present within your life, you will find that everything somehow falls into place, your days run more smoothly, your relationships are enriched and life in general has more flavour.

Inviting the angels into your life is as simple as closing your eyes and saying something like:

Angels, I call you and I invite you into my home and my life.

You will probably come across little signs that your plea has been heard – someone may give you an angel statue as a gift, or you may find a beautiful picture of an angel for your home or a CD of music inspired by angels. The more you open your heart to the angels, the more they will become a part of your life.

Working magick with angelic energies will ensure that your spells work for the highest good of all, and you won't need to worry about any kind of backfire! In addition to all of this, you will come to realise that you have a constant source of love, power and support to turn to and that you are never truly alone.

Creating an angel altar

An altar or shrine dedicated to the angels will create a beautiful focal point within your home and will be a magickal place for you to make contact with your guardian angel and other celestial beings.

First of all, decide where you want your altar to be. Next cover your chosen altar surface with a white or silver cloth. Trim the edges of your altar by pinning in place a white feather boa. Place two glass or silver candlesticks towards the back of the altar and use white or silver candles as your illuminators.

Now decorate the altar so that it represents the angelic elementals it is dedicated to. Obviously, figures of angels are best for this – and they can be bought quite cheaply during the Christmas period. If you have a little extra cash, you might like to invest in a few of the Snow Angel figures that are available from gift shops.

These can be quite expensive but they are very beautiful. Next place a pretty incense or oil burner on your altar and a vase of white flowers. If you have a guardian angel brooch or a set of oracular angel cards for divination, then put these on your altar too. Add pretty items to enhance the beauty of your altar, for example a bowl of clear quartz, snowy quartz and moonstone crystals, or a scattering of white feathers.

Finally, hang a picture of an angel or a pair of decorative angel wings on the wall above your altar. This is now a magickal place for you to commune with the celestial beings of love and light.

Your guardian angel

Everyone has a guardian angel – and I mean everyone! This includes you. While the idea of guardian angels may at first be difficult to digest, if you open your heart and mind and ask the angels to send you a sign of their presence, one will come to you. We will be looking more at this a little later. For now, let's consider the reasons why some of us don't believe in guardian angels.

One reason is that we assume that if we had a guardian angel nothing bad or unpleasant would ever happen to us, right? Wrong! Angels work to one simple rule – they can't interfere in human life unless we ask them to. So unless you ask your guardian angel to help you over an illness or through a difficult time, he's not at liberty to assist you. You must exercise your free will and actually ask for angelic help.

Secondly, we may assume that if the world were watched over by angels and celestial beings, disasters wouldn't happen. This isn't the case because even chaos has its place in the universe, and bad things provide us with lessons to learn from.

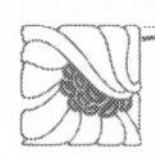

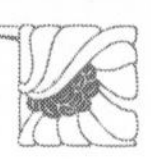

Living through a disaster or great personal tragedy is difficult, to say the least, but again and again what results from the experience is an increased awareness of universal love and compassion and a willingness to help others. This is the angels at work, doing all they can do in such circumstances to keep hope alive and bring people together through love and mutual support.

At such times only the angels and elementals are privy to the bigger picture and can see what lesson humankind is about to learn. So personal tragedy and global disasters should certainly not be seen as evidence that guardian angels don't exist, but evidence of the fact that they do!

Give me a sign!

There are lots of ways for your guardian angel to tap you on the shoulder and introduce himself. Perhaps you've always had a fascination with angels and have filled your home with angel pictures and statues. Maybe someone has given you an angel gift for your birthday or another celebration. Maybe you hear songs about angels whenever you turn on the radio. All of these seemingly everyday things are subtle signs from your guardian angel, who is offering a hand of love and friendship.

Other angelic signs are the sound of bells ringing seemingly out of nowhere, wind chimes tinkling though there is no wind, or the sudden appearance of a dove. If you feel you need proof that you have a guardian angel and that he is listening out for your call, then try this simple exercise.

Sit quietly for a few moments and breathe deeply until you feel calm and centred. Then close your eyes and say out loud:

Guardian angel, hear this plea:
Send me a sign that I may see
That I'm not alone, that you're always near
And that my call you will always hear.

Offer me proof of your shining light
And send me a feather of brilliant white.
So mote it be!

For the next few days keep your eyes peeled. Eventually, you will come across a white feather and you will know that your guardian angel has heard you and is there for you.

Guardian angel invocation

You can invoke the help and assistance of your guardian angel at any time by repeating the invocation below. You can say it at your altar if you wish, but I suggest that you commit the words to memory so that you can call on your angel any time, any place, anywhere!

Close your eyes and bring to mind the image of your guardian angel. Then say the following invocation;

Guardian angel, bring your light;
Make my future days as bright.
Bring with you an angelic shield
As your mighty sword you wield.
Embrace me with protective wings,
Guard me from all harmful things.
I call you here your power to lend
And welcome the love of an angel friend.
So mote it be!

Enhance this invocation by wearing a guardian angel pin or brooch. Repeat as often as you need to.

Angel letters

The idea of writing a letter to your guardian angel may seem strange at first, but it is actually a variation of the ancient art of petition magick, in which a magickal goal or request is written down and then committed to one of the elements, usually Fire, in which case the spell paper is burnt.

In this ritual we take petition magick one step further by writing a detailed letter to the angels. Not only does this offer a mental release from whatever is troubling you but it also allows you to see the situation more clearly as you write about it. And, of course, it ultimately gives your guardian angel the chance to help you out. You can also perform this ritual to express your gratitude.

You will need: A pad of white paper and a silver pen, your brewing pot or a heatproof dish.

Moon phase: Any.

- Go to your angel altar and light the candles. Now sit comfortably and breathe deeply until you feel calm and centred.
- Call on your guardian angel by performing the Guardian Angel Invocation on page 183.
- Breathe deeply again and focus on whatever is troubling you or that you require angelic assistance with (or that you feel grateful for).
- Using the silver pen and white paper, write a letter to your guardian angel expressing all the fear, hurt, worry, anger, despair, love, joy, gratitude and so on that you are feeling right now. Make the letter as honest and detailed as possible, then finish it with the words:

  With love and thanks for your care and support,
  from your charge — (sign your name).

- Read the letter out loud once and then roll it up and light it from one of the illuminator candles. Allow it to burn in the brewing pot or heatproof vessel.
- Remain at your altar for as long as you wish, then blow out the candles and go about your day. The spell is now complete and you should have evidence of angelic assistance very soon.

Archangel circle of protection

This is a great protection spell, calling angelic forces to guard you on all sides. Use it on its own or in conjunction with the Guardian Angel Invocation on page 183. Again, I suggest that you learn the calls in this spell by heart so that you always have access to them. If you wish, you can also use this spell to invoke the angel of each quarter to guard your magick circle.

You will need: Nothing.
Moon phase: Any.

- Face north, raise both arms high above your head and, visualising the archangel Uriel, say:

I call on Uriel, angel of the north,
Angel of magick and dreams, protector of witches.
I call you here to protect and guide me.

- Face east, raise both arms high above your head and, visualising the archangel Raphael, say:

I call on Raphael, angel of the east,
Light bearer and divine healer.
I call you here to protect and guide me.

- Face south, raise both arms high above your head and, visualising the archangel Michael, say:

I call on Michael, angel of the south,
Angel of justice, valour and strength.
I call you here to protect and guide me.

- Face west, raise both arms high above your head and, visualising the archangel Gabriel, say:

I call on Gabriel, angel of the west,
Protector of women and children, bringing peace to all.
I call you here to protect and guide me.
So mote it be!

You are now protected by the strongest angelic forces.

Angel hugs

Sometimes even the strongest person needs a hug, and nothing could be more uplifting than the embrace of an angel. Whenever you are feeling a little down or lonely, or if you've had a bad day, call on the angels and ask for a hug! You can perform this little spell anywhere you need to – at work, in the supermarket, in your car – but if you're at home, go to your angel altar. Your angel is always right beside you, waiting for your call.

You will need: Nothing

Moon phase: Any – use when required.

- Close your eyes and breathe deeply, then visualise your guardian angel and say:

  Guardian angel, hear this plea;
  In love and trust I call on thee.
  Embrace me with your feathered wings
  And give me strength to face all things.
  At this time I need a hug;
  Please fill me with your peace and love.
  So mote it be!

- Remain seated and wait for your angel's embrace. As soon as you feel warm and calm, you will know that you are enfolded in your angel's wings. You may also feel a tingling sensation or a shiver down your spine as your energies merge with those of your angel. Soak up your angel's loving strength.

Afterword

And so we come to the end of our journey together. I hope that you have enjoyed our little trip through the Enchanted Realm and that you have found spells and exercises in this book to interest and inspire you.

We have looked at the magickal powers of gnomes, sylphs, salamanders, sirens, dryads, elves, pixies, satyrs and angels. We have discovered the deeper magick of faerie tales and found new relevance in ancient myths. But even so, we have only touched the tip of the iceberg. Faerie magick and folklore is a vast subject, and I hope that you continue to study the Enchanted Realm in your own way. I also hope that you will go on to read my previous books, which will enable you to study magick and witchcraft in all its wonderful diversity!

In the meantime, may your life be a magickal faerie tale and may you live happily ever after! Farewell my magickal reader, until our next merry meeting.

With love and bright blessings to you all,

Morgana

Further Reading

By the same author:

Candleburning Rituals, Quantum/Foulsham
Everyday Spells for a Teenage Witch, Quantum/Foulsham
The Witch's Almanac, Quantum/Foulsham
Magical Beasts, Quantum/Foulsham
How to Create a Magical Home, Quantum/Foulsham
First Steps to Solitary Witchcraft, Quantum/Foulsham

Books on faeries and folklore:

Katherine Briggs, *A Book of Fairies,* Penguin Books, 1977
David Day, *The Quest for King Arthur,* De Agostini Editions, 1995
Lori Eisenkraft-Palazzola, *Fairies,* Smithmark Publishers, 1999
Lori Eisenkraft-Palazzola, *Witches,* Smithmark Publishers, 1999
Joseph Jacobs, *Celtic Fairy Tales,* Leopard/Random House, 1995
Claire Nahmad, *Fairy Spells,* Souvenir Press, 1997

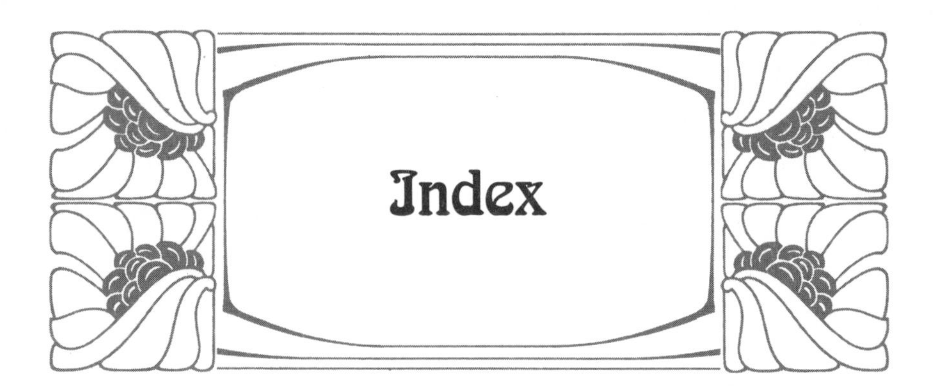

Index

Spells are written in *italics*. **Bold** type indicates major page references.

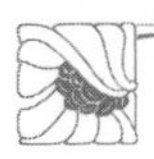

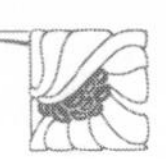

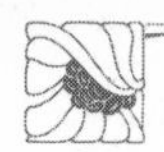

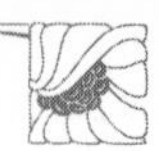